SOMETIMES IT'S FUNNY:
ADVENTURES IN PARENTHOOD

EA and JA FLOOD

Conscious Dreams
PUBLISHING

Sometimes It's Funny: Adventures in Parenthood

Copyright © 2025: EA and JA Flood

All rights reserved. No part of this publication may be produced, distributed, or transmitted in any form or by any means, including photocopying, recording, or other electronic or mechanical methods, without the prior written permission of the publisher, except in the case of brief quotations embodied in critical reviews and certain other non-commercial uses permitted by copyright law.

Published by Conscious Dreams Publishing
www.consciousdreamspublishing.com

Book Consultant Daniella Blechner

Edited by Elise Abram

Cover Design by Emily's World of Design

Typeset by Oksana Kosovan

ISBN: 978-1-917584-23-4

For Jahdiel

A merry heart doeth good like a medicine.
– Proverbs 17:22 KJV

Contents

- 7   Thinking...
- 21   You're Married...Where's The Baby?
- 35   Two Worlds
- 45   The Birth
- 55   Where's The Manual?
- 73   Kiss at the Bars and All Those Ahhh Moments
- 89   Musical Interlude
- 101   Sleep!
- 115   Child Care
- 147   Every Hair on Your Head
- 159   Is It Enough?
- 173   ...With Thanks
- 185   About the Authors

Thinking...

Do not despise these small beginnings,
for the Lord rejoices to see the work begin.
- Zechariah 4:10 NLT

Edward's Interlude

MUSIC PLAYS IN MY HEAD AND I SMILE. I think of some of the many songs my son Jahdiel likes to sing or that we like to play to him. As I sit on the train winging its way to the coast, I think of our own journey, the three of us. So much to think about. Multi-layered. Almost overwhelming at times. Grown men do not cry, apparently, but the traitorous tears in my eyes as I reflect betray that mantra.

When I was younger, I thought about what the future might hold. I made certain assumptions about what and who would be in my life. The cup runneth over reality is sublime; yes, it is, even with all the nonsense this life journey may bring.

One of the superpowers Jahdiel has is to erase the nonsense or at least park it hurriedly, albeit temporarily, in the kiss-my-teeth section of the brain.

As the train meanders its way through the English countryside, farmhouses peek through the trees, and I wonder whether we—I—have been overthinking the process. It has been really hard not to overthink it, of course. Responsible as you are for an actual human being, you fight to make sure every micro decision does not transform, morph into issues that a therapist has to unpack. I critically analyse what I have done so far in the same way we used to critically analyse novels and poetry during English Literature A-Level at the London Oratory School. What did that phrase mean in Act 2, Scene 4, line 162? Did the author really mean that?

Through it all, it really has been an adventure. I've discovered more of who I am and what I value because of my journey thus far with Jahdiel.

It is because I have had to think.

Thinking

We realised we had two stories in one. True, Josi, my wife, and I are raising Jahdiel together, and our impressions and reactions are often similar. Interesting, is it not though, that the same incident can be seen and felt in different ways by different people, that different meanings and significances can be derived from the same episode? That experiences are not and cannot always be experienced the same? Why make two voices artificially one, when they can sit together to make harmonious music?

So, I started these conversations, and Josi had oversight. She reflected. I was fine with that. It helped with a fuller perspective, I think.

I was not always at peace with her wifely oversight, of course. The first memorable and obvious time she checked my work was when Jahdiel was only a few months old, though my memories, in general, are mostly in black and white, fading with time. Like a photograph slowly fading and blurring unless touched up by current events, the colours are not exact.

But no, that memory of my work being checked is in technicolour. I remember it very well. Josi, Jahdiel and I were in his bedroom. It was a small room. His cot was on one side opposite the large window, so it could be bathed in light as needed or covered when not. The walls were a tasteful neutral colour. There was a matching wardrobe and chest set nestled along the third wall. His teal chair was along the fourth wall, placed at just the right angle to see through the door into the hallway and, with a slight movement of the eyes, to see fully into his room. Yes, it was all planned. Each item was barely a few months older than Jahdiel himself. There was the smell of newness in the room, battling (and losing) against the fragrance of the newness of Jahdiel.

I was changing his nappy on the floor of his bedroom. The thick cream carpet — yes, cream! — was so spongy that the changing mat hardly seemed needed. I was fairly confident with that aspect of fatherhood, even a few months in. I rather expertly removed the soiled nappy, careful to raise his legs at just the right angle. I had no idea whether there was an optimum angle, but I assumed there must be one within a narrow margin of error. Whatever. I was firmly within the leg-raising optimum angle and removed the soiled nappy.

The clean nappy lovingly put on, I smiled haughtily at Josi, and she smiled back. Clearly, if there was a nappy changing trophy to be had, my name was likely being etched on it as we spoke. Perhaps from the nappy-changing Olympics, I mused.

I had come so far by that time. Before Jahdiel, I had changed a grand total of one nappy on an actual real baby, not counting the practice runs during the ante-natal classes with the baby doll. At Josi's baby shower, a family member

Thinking

attended with one of my godchildren. That was another presumption of mine dashed: men can apparently attend baby showers. My godchild was a few months old – it was the perfect opportunity for some last-minute cramming before the real event of our own baby.

'Go on,' our cousin Jackie said. 'You change his nappy.'

'Okay,' I replied, wandering off to the end of the room farthest away from the others at the party. Their eyes followed me across the room, which was not big enough to have enough furniture for hiding behind.

I really did not need to have an audience, but I soldiered on. Seconds passed. Very conscious of the many eyes on me, I felt the heat of their various emotions. Beads of sweat snaked down my brow, keen to see which of them would pass over my eyes and down to my clearly-too-thick polo neck jumper. I panicked as I tried to put the theoretical training I had into practice. My godchild looked up at me with – I felt sure – pity in his eyes. 'This is the first and last time,' he was clearly thinking, and actually, it would be. It seemed like torture (to me, not to him), as some helpful person video-recorded the event. That video needed to remain buried, but I did it; mission accomplished.

Fast forward back to that technicolour moment when I successfully and expertly changed Jahdiel's nappy. My brow was bone dry. Confidence was high as I made my way from the bedroom to the bathroom to wash my hands. My back could not be straighter. The bathroom was in a direct line of sight from Jahdiel's room. It was a bright morning. If there were birds around, they would have been singing. I like to think it would have been Bob Marley's 'Three Little Birds'.

I turned and glanced back into Jahdiel's room on my way to complete the washing of the hands routine.

Froze.

Wait. She – no! Did she just re-adjust the nappy? Yes, my contact lenses were in, so there was no mistaking it. You hear people talking about time standing still and think what nonsense, but yes, there was such a thing. Time advanced in slow motion. Stood still. Then the world crashed back in, and I continued on my way to the bathroom.

We never spoke of the incident.

I laugh now.

Now.

Then and at other times, perhaps my work did need to be checked, but now I see it for what it was: teamwork. There I am, thinking again. You see, it cannot be helped. We have a huge respect for those who do not have a team to help raise one child, never mind more than one child. Team Flood was absolutely necessary to raise Jahdiel, and Josi was the one who made sure our teamwork was on track.

Earlier, I said that I started these conversations, but why should the father be the one to start? Fathers are increasingly taking a more active role in child care, stepping into the forefront rather than remaining in the background. According to research,[1] there has been a significant decline in the proportion of people who believe the best way of arranging work and caring for young children is for the mother to stay at home and the father to work full-time. This research looks at the change in British social and political attitudes over the last 40 years. Its data points towards attitudes moving in the direction of a more egalitarian outlook on gender roles, with couples sharing responsibility for working and caring. Interestingly, much of the public from whom the data was collected cling to the view that family, rather than public daycare, should be where pre-school children are looked after. The research found that people still expect mothers to hold the main responsibility for providing care to young children — all very interesting stuff.

I had seen for myself, from my own non-exhaustive 'daddy research', that I was in good dad company. The times I took Jahdiel to nursery in the morning, pulled him along on his scooter like I was his hired help (and I was), it is clear that dads were getting stuck in with all aspects of the nursery run. Children were brought by dads

---

[1] Allen, J. & Stevenson, I. (2023, September 21). *BSA 40: Gender Roles*. National Centre for Social Research. https://natcen.ac.uk/publications/bsa-40-gender-roles

in various ways: holding toddlers' hands on the way to nursery or school, carrying toddlers around on their necks or backs, on bikes and strapping them on in front or from behind. Baby carriers and toddlers in strollers, two babies in strollers, toddlers on scooters, freed dads to scoot a baby mile (10 metres), and on and on. It is for this reason that the narrative you are reading, co-chaired by a dad, should come as no surprise.

There are benefits all round for fathers to step forward, it seems. Some of the key findings in another piece of research[2] include that the fathers' involvement in childcare improves children's emotional well-being, cognitive development and academic achievement and is good for the fathers themselves. The same review also found that the equal division of childcare and housework between couples helped reduce parental stress, especially for mothers and increased relationship satisfaction, thus decreasing the likelihood of divorce or relationship dissolution. A lot of this seems fairly obvious when said out loud, but it is great to have statistics and details to back up the assumptions. Little did I know at the time that my seemingly innocent jaunts to nursery would come with such positive ripples.

---

2 Chung, H. (2021). *Shared care, father's involvement in care and family well-being outcomes: Literature review*. Report for the Government Equalities Office. London: UK Cabinet Office.

Thinking

So, a significant proportion of parents bringing babies and toddlers to nurseries were fathers. So much so that when, on occasion, a mum would bring little Johnny to nursery I scrutinised her, mentally listing all the ways her pram technique and goodbye to Johnny were different than Dad's. I wondered why the picture of Mum with little Johnny seemed strangely odd, then realised it was because I was not used to seeing mothers doing the nursery run.

It was from these small beginnings that passion was ignited—the little day-to-day events of getting on with parenting, passion for the world of babies and blessings, toddlers and toys—setting free a side of you that you did not know existed. It didn't just bring out my nurturing side, but my fiercely protective side, too!

I now understood more about what Gandalf meant when he proclaimed, 'You will not pass!' I will be his protection. Your negativity will not get to him through the barrier that is me, so I proclaim to you that you will not pass my child. You will not stop him, hamper him, confine him, define him. I have to do enough for him. The world needs to do enough for him.

As I sit on the train winging its way through the English countryside, I cannot help but smile again at the many things Jahdiel has said and done. Then I laugh and laugh. Out loud! The old lady in the seat across from mine looks at me with suspicion. I feel the heat of her stare as an almost physical force. I look directly at her during a gap in my laughter and my smile widens. Momentarily stunned at the unexpected reaction to what she no doubt thought was her projection of a dressing down, she smiles back, then chuckles, which lights up her face. The frowning wrinkles are pleasantly rearranged on her face to accommodate her current pleasure as she turns away. Momentarily in sync, we both look out of our respective windows as the countryside races by.

The next stop is mine.

Josi's Reflections

I LISTEN INTENTLY FOR ANY NOISE COMING FROM UPSTAIRS. Yes, Jahdiel is still asleep. I pull the blanket further around myself, and my eye catches a picture on the blanket of me holding him when he was a baby. We were at Cousin Melrose's birthday party. I think it was one of the very first parties we attended as a family with Jahdiel. My eyes glance over the array of photographs of me on the blanket. There are a number of them covering the whole of one side of the blanket, the other side a pleasant light blue reflecting the cold perhaps but also calming. The blanket was a birthday present said to represent the twin bastions of memories

Thinking

and warmth. As winter approaches, the latter, I think, is winning the battle for priority.

The television grabs my attention again. Co-pastor Penny Francis is preaching at the Sapphire Women's Conference 2023. Her text was 1 Samuel 1, verse 1 to 9: Elkanah and his two wives, Hannah and Peninnah. Peninnah had children, but Hannah had no children. While Elkanah loved Hannah, the Lord had shut up her womb. Peninnah would provoke Hannah to make her worry, fret and cry because the Lord had shut up her womb. Hannah did not eat, such was her feeling about the situation. Elkanah asked Hannah why she was crying, why was she not eating and why her heart grieved.

Scripture says it best: 'She wept, and did not eat. Then said Elkanah, her husband, to her, "Hannah, why weepest thou? And why eatest thou not? And why is thy heart grieved? Am not I better to thee than ten sons?"'

Co-pastor Penny Francis tells the story of when she gave birth to her second child. She tells the story of having a caesarean and the multitude of emotions wrapped up in having a baby on top of the practicalities and complications that can come with having a caesarean. She thought it would be a usual birth. She lay on the hospital bed, exhausted physically and mentally, while her husband, Bishop John Francis, cradles their baby girl. The smiles on his face—I imagine these as plural smiles—the excitement and pride in his countenance threatens to extinguish all other feelings in the room. When Co-pastor Penny Francis gets home, she starts to cry: the exhaustion, the weariness, the everything. Whatever it is, and she does not know it at the time, it is all too much.

'What's wrong with you?' her husband asks.

'Sometimes,' says Co-pastor Penny Francis, looking into the camera, 'the men do not understand. They just do not get it. Maybe later they do, or will.'

'You will see when you hold your baby in your arms,' so said my general practitioner, Dr Melissa, on a routine visit many years ago, before Jahdiel came along. Sometimes, the reality of the present seems so far removed from my younger self that it is laughable. Could I please go back in time and say to my younger self it is well? Not only that it will be well, but it IS well. Can I remind my younger self that He's got you as He's always got you? Dr Melissa's words, the confirmation they were, buoyed me along until the reality of Jahdiel came through, the in-your-face reality of the expectations we put on ourselves and the expectations of others and how those twin expectations feed into each other.

The first child and wanting – no, needing – to get it right. Including changing the nappy of the tiny, young person on our bed, touching him so lightly, doing what, in quick time, became an everyday task that I hardly touched him at all. Initially feeling that the baby camera was all over the house.

Thinking

Big Brother was watching, and he was Aunty X, Uncle Y, Cousin A, Cousin B and FamilyFriends I did not yet know as such. Carrying the rucksack, I would slowly, slowly hand over, as the battle was not mine.

With the featheriest of touches, I would readjust that nappy that Edward had put on our son, because it had to be right. I would later learn of the army of family and friends who had also walked this journey. Later.

I nod to Co-pastor Penny Francis through the airwaves and smile with her. I know and can share in the mix of nerves and emotions of which she speaks, when she talks about the experiences of having her children. I reflect on the thankfulness of being brought through the process, the journey so far on the good ship *Flood*. I pull up the blanket towards my chin and continue listening and thinking.

You're Married... Where's The Baby?

And God blessed them, and God said unto them, Be fruitful, and multiply, and replenish the earth, and subdue it.
– **Genesis 1:28 KJV**

We had many discussions about children before getting engaged; obviously. There would be no children before marriage; obviously. It was one of the Big Things to talk about going into the marriage and was not a discussion we thought could or should be avoided. That is not to say that the engagement was put on hold pending the successful completion of the negotiations surrounding children, but there was an unspoken feeling that it was one of those Big Things that had to be discussed and decided upon, those things about which we had to say I do before we could say I Do.

There were dual bastions that assisted us going into our union, which would feature children. The first was couple's pre-marriage counselling. Who knew that counselling could come before cracks—that would become crevices that could become craters—could develop? Who knew that counselling would let you squint into the distance to see the road that led to those micro blows that would wear you down so you would take another road? Clearly, many people do to have such a creature exist as couple's pre-marriage counselling.

Second was a couple's book given to us by the Drysdales; the same book times two: one for me and one for Josi. We read the same chapter separately as instructed and then came together to discuss what it said. English Literature A Level comes to mind again. That trite statement, you do not know what you do not know, the one that was tempting to try to ban from vocabularies everywhere as it falls into the 'painfully obvious' box, was actually on point. Those books are now stock presents from us to couples intending to marry. Sorry, but now that we know, I moved on from providing engraved wine glasses as wedding presents.

So, we spoke of little Jahdiels before we ever knew of Jahdiel. Let us not say who wanted more children; suffice to say that someone (okay—hand up: it was me) envisioned a version of 'Come to me my children' as a swarm of progeny dutifully make their way to Papa with a smile fixed on Papa's face. Fast forward 25 to 30 years, and they would all be firmly established in a profession. Of course, Child A would be a doctor, Child B would be a lawyer, Child C would be the top of something or another and Child D would decide to do something artsy, that type of thing. I was raised in Saint Lucia and Josi in Montserrat, so we knew, practically instinctively, that there really were only three prime choices: lawyer, doctor or other. So, those are your choices, dutiful progeny as yet unnamed; pick one. No problem if you want to change professions—pick another one from the list.

We did not enjoy married life for long before other people started querying, enquiring and showing downright rudeness when it came to when we might have children. I do not think this came from malice—people cannot seem to grapple with the idea of being married and not having children. Being fruitful and multiplying is also about your skills and talents, is it not? About the positive impact you have on this world? Perhaps even more so. How have you made your one talent into three or more? Have you hidden it away to waste? That whole concept is completely ignored. A lot of times, people just feel the need to make conversation, and the post-marriage-children-chat seems an obvious hit. Then again, who was I to criticise, given that the children conversation was at the forefront of our minds long before marriage? If it was so important to us, why shouldn't it be to those around us?

It all started off with a light touch: 'You look so good together; you'll make lovely parents.' A popular comment.

'Enjoy your married life; babies will come later,' a few said.

The smiles accompanying these statements found their mirror in our faces. If I were the right hue to blush, I would as I basked in those well-meaning compliments. There was no need for heating in those autumn evenings as the warm sentiments from our family and friends kept us cosy and glowing.

That state of being can, however, only last so long. Slowly but surely, the number of teeth accompanying the smiles from family and friends started to decrease until they disappeared altogether, the tone of their statements on all things baby became less jolly, and uncertainty started to creep into their eyes. 'Are they having problems?' seemed to project from their thoughts. You think you are imagining things until you notice that the sparkle in their eyes has become less, well, sparkly.

Months passed, and the tone became more direct, insistent: 'Lovely couple—when are we going to see baby?' said the speaker as they continued dancing past during offering time in church.

'Good child-bearing hips,' proclaimed a well-intentioned older aunt as she gave Josi a whack on each hip as if to emphasise the point or point out, in case we were unaware, the body parts of which she spoke.

That was a state of being that began to annoy. It started to get predictable as to which conversation Person A would start or Person B would end. It was a state of being that could be considered humorous, but only in hindsight.

Our own smiles became more strained.

Then, the helpful pointers progressed to the aforementioned rudeness: 'You're not getting any younger!' The smile from the proclaimer, while delivering the blindingly obvious statement, did nothing to dent the sting in the words. No, it was not funny, actually.

By then, our smiles were plastic, manufactured just for Ms and Mr Rude. They should have been grateful that our ages had given us just enough wisdom for our reaction to be those manufactured plastic smiles.

So, I bit my tongue. I did not say, 'You are also not getting any younger,' to Persons A and B. I did not tell them a little bit about themselves as others might have done.

Actually, we were used to the direct approach. When you grew up with people who keep pointing out the obvious, like, 'You really have spots on your face,' (Oh, is that what they are?), or an older relative providing some (un)helpful advice, 'You're really getting fat — don't you have time for the gym?' you soon learnt to develop a thick skin and put on your armour as they approached. They really did not mean it the way it might have leapt off the page. They were not the crushing blows they might seem, which would have necessitated taking them off from the Christmas list and never speaking to them again. No. That was just how our family and friends have always been. In fact, their silence would have seemed out of the ordinary. Silence would have been louder than their spoken words.

What you must do is insulate yourself against feeling as if you are having a baby just for the tick. Marriage: tick. Home: tick. Good times: tick. Fun: tick. Baby: tick—the catalogue of unspoken things you are expected to do on someone else's list. Clearly, those well-intentioned people will be there to help in due course, like they are with all of their other well-intentioned suggestions. That is the unspoken hope and expectation; time will tell.

To be fair to these unnamed persons, the topic of a baby started as early as the wedding day. We got married in Saint Lucia, island paradise, Helen of the West. That Saint Lucia is an island paradise is not biased—when you know a place, you have inside information and can say what is great and what is not. Saint Lucia, with its drive-in volcano, Sulphur Springs, Diamond Falls, iconic Petit Piton and Gros Piton and friendly people. As you travelled on the aeroplane from your home destination to Saint Lucia, you looked out of the window, eager for a first glimpse of the island. You saw lush green vegetation, undulating hills and pockets of buildings dotted around. The vegetation so full, the colours so vibrant it was almost too much for an eye so used to monotone dullness. As the aeroplane descended on the tarmac, you felt the weight of work, stress and worry ascend from your shoulders. That weight returned when you left the island, but for now, it was elsewhere. The door of the aeroplane opened, and you were greeted by warm air. It smelled fresh, new, like no one has ever used that portion of air before. You smiled not even realising you were smiling; you were home.

We got married at Sandals Grande in the north of the island. It was a beautiful day. Sunny but not too hot. Josi looked gorgeous, walking down the aisle in the open air as the wonderful Caribbean Sea breeze met the Atlantic Ocean breeze, decided they'd work well together and gently tried to lift Josi's veil.

I cried.

Josi sang to me during the reception.

I cried. I had to hydrate myself with the amount of crying I did on that day.

At least two people giving speeches spoke about having babies; twins, suggested one. We all laughed uproariously, but really, babies were not uppermost in our minds as we celebrated and danced and laughed, completely immersed in our two families coming together. Some had met for the very first time. People connected or reconnected. The bar was free, and so were the good times. No, babies were not on the carefully drafted schedule for the wedding day. Even if they were, I would have had to hand the baby conversations over to our mistress of ceremony, Cousin Germaine, just like I had to give her the wedding day schedule.

We walked down the aisle, basking in the bliss of the unknown of what, exactly, would come when Jahdiel arrived.

After the wedding, the months passed. We exchanged glances with fellow newlyweds, sharing that sweet period after the wedding but before children. Children moved from being the furthest thing from our minds on our wedding day to the front and centre. Together with those other newlywed couples, we walked the path that took us, in time, to the pregnancy test. Of course, we remembered the date of the particular test for the pregnancy that would become Jahdiel. We still have a picture of the test kit. The intention to chronicle every single precious moment while it was still fresh. I had just come back from a jog, and the results were waiting for me when I got home, sitting on the Bible.

I welled up — hydration doubly required.

We took a moment to take it in and appreciate the wonder of it all.

There were loads of people out there with children; that has always clearly been the case, but that seemed new to me now. I went from being only vaguely aware of seeing any children around me to suddenly thinking that children were all there was in the world. Everywhere. The full spectrum. Where had they all come from? Maybe it was a trick of the eye and brain glossing over what was not desperately or even mildly important to me at the time that prevented me from seeing them. Then began a proper interest in those amazing creatures.

It's a different world when you are going to have a baby. You seem to enter into the inner circle.

Would our baby turn out to be like that one? Please, not like that one! Please, please, not like the one having a wobbly in the supermarket aisle. Time passed. Sensibility descended. We just wanted a healthy baby, thank you. The rest would take care of itself because it had to.

We chose not to find out the baby's gender before birth. There seemed so few things that were pleasantly surprising in this life's journey that we wanted one of those moments. Getting emotionally ready was one thing; getting the space ready in our home was something else, entailing a lot of visits to various baby stores. Those institutions of babyhood held no interest for me before, except for the odd visit to buy a present for a godchild or child-related event. The colours, range and choice were overwhelming; the talk about the best kind of pushchair, the optimal folding variety or lightweight kind, baby carriers, yes or no, specially made for such or something that looks like a long, large scarf for which a PhD was required to navigate effectively.

Then came the choosing of a name. We opted for a biblical one, so we both separately created a short list of boys' and girls' names, then we got together and whittled it down to one boy's name and one girl's.

'Suppose he or she does not look like the name you choose?' a friend asked. Well, whether he or she looked like that or not, it would be his or her name! As it happened, Jahdiel, which means 'whom God makes glad', fit into his name, so we did not have a crisis moment, worrying if his chosen name fit him or not.

You wonder about children being given names that are layered with connotations, either for good or for ill. Will he or she naturally grow into that name, or will they force themself into the name, feeling they have no choice? What do you do if you are named 'Pharoah'?

A close friend to the you're-married-now-where's-the-baby narrative is, 'When is the little one going to get a little sister?' You've come into another buzzing of the well-intended, irrespective of your own hopes, intentions or, indeed, pocket, irrespective of the reality of your situation, and the dance started all over again with a different slant. But that was for another day.

You're Married...Where's The Baby

Josi's Reflections

THE FORCE OF THE EXPECTATION OFTEN DID NOT REQUIRE SPOKEN WORDS. I saw the quiet many who spoke no words and were the louder for it. The weight of an island, Montserrat; the Emerald Isle of the Caribbean. Was there something in its name, Montserrat, meaning a jagged or serrated mountain? Growing up in Montserrat, the youngest of the cousins and spoiled for it, I thought about what I should bring with me when I made the journey to the United Kingdom as a young girl. I did not know that the golden sunshine would not make its way through immigration, nor would a childhood free of care. I did not know that hidden deep in my suitcase, so deep it would only be found many years later, was a piece of cultural code that made it clear that babies would follow marriage, a path as inevitable as the rivers making their way to the sea I loved so much. Annoying as it may be, frustrating as it may be — or maybe even sweet — it was the unspoken reality. The feelings surrounding it were, frankly, irrelevant.

I had a dear friend in the United Kingdom many years later who got married at what many would consider an advanced age. She had the timeless youth of the Lord, so no one knew her age. It was an age that, however forceful the expectation, bore wisdom and grace and so many wonderful things, but not a child. Did she ever dare tell the community how she felt about the expectation that had been placed on her that would never be realised? Did she have to face a well-intentioned older aunt who thought her gynaecoid pelvis was fit for purpose? That aunt who'd echoed an even older aunt, who'd spun me round as if approving of a specimen to be taken to market? It was funny then, as it is funny now, the humour tinged with what? Should we call it expectation again?

It was, therefore, refreshing to have those very few people who spoke a different narrative, those precious few voices who would give the wise counsel that I—we—should enjoy our marriage before we thought of children. There was no need to rush; the babies would come. They knew that once the fragile being came, he would take over, and the focus then for both of us parents would be on him. While few and far between, these sentiments comforted me like a cool breeze. It felt like that same breeze that sang with me as I belted out song after song on top of the hill next to my grandmother's house in Montserrat, that beautiful emerald with its majestic mountains.

Those precious few voices carried me to the now delightful expectation of having a healthy baby who would be a combination of Edward and me. That would be a blessing. And the baby would come in His own time. Meanwhile, we gave Ms and Mr Rude our plastic smiles because we were smiling on the inside, enjoying the journey on the way to its destination. I smile again now, thinking how interesting it is that others do not tell you of their own journey to baby. Only afterwards, when you share your tales, do they share their own. It is only then that they speak of being told what to eat and what not to eat, alternative remedies and acupuncture, being told to think about freezing their eggs, just in case, all in the desperate quest to have a baby. It is only when I join their club that they share their own stories of before they joined the club themselves.

And so, I cast my mind back to that Saturday morning of the pregnancy test. Edward was out jogging. Holding my breath, I waited to see whether the double lines appeared, smiling in shock when they did. All I could think was, 'Oh, wow!' I was overwhelmed and desperately wanted to share the precious moment with Edward, but I knew he would not be back for 45 minutes. Forty-five minutes of complex emotion for the child for which we had prayed. Forty-five minutes in which I was the only one in the world who knew, swimming in an ocean of possibilities. I placed the test on the Bible for his return.

I smiled as Edward opened the door.

Two Worlds

I have learned, in whatsoever state I am, therewith to be content. I know both how to be abased, and I know how to abound: every where and in all things I am instructed both to be full and to be hungry, both to abound and to suffer need.
– Philippians 4:11-12 KJV

THE WORLD IS DIVIDED INTO TWO: BEFORE CHILD AND AFTER CHILD. I know that. Now. I remember the first world, Before Child, blissfully unaware of what was on the other side of the threshold. In fact, not even aware that there were two worlds. Those parents and their children were on the fringe of my world, but nevertheless a part of it. I went to work, went to the cinema, ate out with friends, and they did the same, just with that extra bit: the child.

I had been exposed to that other world, of course, visiting friends and relatives with babies and toddlers. Those times were deluged with everything baby, looking desperately for some oasis, some reprieve from the unrelenting... well, baby-ness.

'Yes, the baby is very cute,' I would feel obliged to comment to a parent or relative whenever a so-called bundle of joy was thrust in my direction.

'He does, indeed, look like his mother, but with his father's smile,' I would continue since the comment about his cuteness was clearly insufficient.

'That is grandma's chin, for sure,' I would say in agreement with another parent.

'I agree that smirk really isn't gas but a knowing smile,' I would add, trying to dial down the sarcasm.

'She must be thinking deep thoughts, indeed.'

I rolled my eyes again and again, checking my watch to see whether it was time to leave yet another child-related event and escape. I noticed only 10 minutes had passed by—really? Was that all?

At one such event, I brought my sister (who would later morph into Aunty Dawn) and a cousin as backup. My thinking was that they could be used as a convenient reason to make a quick escape. They had an occasion they just could not be late for, so we could not stay long as a cover story. We arranged a signal in case an escape was not

Two Worlds

needed, escape being the default position. It was all worked out. There were, of course, smiles on our faces as I pressed the doorbell. Our smiles were genuine, as we were pleased on that happy occasion. Just in case, I increased my smile sparkle dial just a notch for the special occasion.

The home was stuffed with well-wishing family and friends, all genuinely happy for the new parents. My gift for the newborn perched precariously on the only available bit of space in the sea of baby paraphernalia. Little did I know that the wobble of the gift, the judgement of gravity as of yet undecided, would reflect a greater social wobble: I did not realise that the shortened version of the child's name, which suggested a boy, hid the actual name of the baby girl. There could not be blame allocated to me. It was, I insisted, a deliberate ploy to embarrass the uninitiated. Too preoccupied with the cuteness-conversation, I did not notice the surreptitious text from my sister warning me, 'It's a girl!' It was too late to retract the boy-blue card, which made its unerring way into the hands of the new mother.

I can still see the scene now in slow motion, and I cringe.

Of course, there have been godchildren who have given me exposure to a world I had yet to be a part of. I had dipped my toe into childcare the odd hour and day (okay, the odd overnight) with them. And yes, yes, of course, it was a pleasure and a privilege to be chosen as a godparent to fill in the gap if anything were to happen to the parents, to be there for the birthdays, the Christmases, for childcare as and when needed. To dip hand in pocket for gifts that were clearly my ideas of what my godchildren should have rather than what they needed or perhaps even wanted. I was completely oblivious as to the ultimate destination of the monster trucks, the colouring pencils, the Wii, the Xbox, the flotsam and the jetsam. Where were they now, that sea of well-intended children's gifts? Hopefully, they have long since been rehoused, passed down to others instead of languishing in the attic, basement, garage or, dare I say, rubbish bin.

Back then, in Before Child World, my view was clear: children should have toys for Christmases and birthdays. It mattered not that there were two (or three) of the very same remote-controlled truck or doll. Surely, that was just double (or triple) the fun. That was written somewhere as a rule, and if not, it should be. What child wants to tear excitedly through Rudolf the reindeer wrapping paper, the passion of the season written all over their adoring faces, only to look down on a pack of socks, slightly too big (they will grow into it), and underwear (you are a big boy now)? What new level of cruelty was that?

Those fleeting experiences of babies and toddlers were all loans. I have already read that book, thank you. No, I do not need to hold onto it any longer. It's a great book, but it is not mine and can go back now. Yes, now. I would be more

Two Worlds

than happy to have the pleasure of a day trip or overnight when the cute little fellow was fully potty trained. The song was right: 'Almost Doesn't Count'.

Back I went to proper sleep, only to be interrupted by late-night work, late-night socialising or husband-and-wife movie night. Little did I know that the sleep I enjoyed was being banked for when I needed to make small or large withdrawals from those sleep memories. When interrupted sleep came as it did, I thought back to those years I'd enjoyed sleep and realised that that, too, shall pass as it was not always like this.

After Child — now, there was an adventure. The world of nurseries and nannies, nappies and night-times, hair and harassment, sleep and slings. However many people describe it, you cannot really truly understand the experience until After Child. We often pondered why people did not tell us about certain aspects of parenthood, but telling and experiencing were very much different things. There was so much to say, so much to tell, deciding where to begin, what should be said and what should not be shared.

The idea of sharing our adventure first came to us during our NCT (National Childbirth Trust) ante-natal classes, hugely useful classes. We learnt so much there. There was only so much that web searches — which we did — would reveal. Going through the learning process with other first-time parents was invaluable, and we are still in contact with some of the parents. Going through something so major together fosters a degree of bonding. We were in the trenches together.

We also wanted to see what it would be like in the state-funded ante-natal classes. Any assistance that prepared us for being parents was welcome. The small library of books that had squeezed their way onto our bookshelf could also only take us so far. Wedged as they were between science fiction and fantasy books and those on Christian living, they threatened to outnumber those on leisure and interest. The books knew the reality that baby would increasingly be our leisure and interest.

So, there we sat, listening and engaging in the NCT classes. We sat in the church hall in a circle, facing each other, a secret society, eager to learn about how it would all happen. I had driven past that same church hall perhaps hundreds of times, not knowing that all things baby had been soaked into its walls, biding their time before bringing us into the fold. I chose not to imagine that we were the first to use it and spoil the image of generations of parents sitting where we sat, being enlightened.

All of our rucksacks contained the various bits and pieces that were suggested we bring in the email pack. We looked round the group and noticed that we were the only couple of African or Caribbean descent in the group of eight couples, but so what? Frankly, it reflected the area in which we lived. But this was London! It did make us wonder, as we had more sessions, whether the information was culturally aware. Was it appropriate for our culture? Did it even need to be? How did you know if something was missing if you did not know? Easy—a family member slapped it in your face in the Montserratian-Saint Lucian way that left you in no doubt!

These were interesting questions, but we parked the idea of further exploration as we got on with the business of having and caring for our baby. It came back to the fore when we realised the absolute adventure of having a child. It was a roller-coaster ride and so funny in parts, although sometimes, only in hindsight, as many things often are. Everything has its season. I am content—no, happy—to be in the second world.

Josi's Reflections

SEISMIC SHIFT. The volcano at Soufriere Hills in Montserrat made its presence definitively known in 1995. It destroyed more than half of the island. Or maybe it was better said that more than half of Montserrat was still there, just buried under lava. Montserratians fled to various parts of the globe. The United Kingdom was an obvious destination for some; we were British citizens, after all, nestled—we thought comfortably—in the Caribbean.

I had moved to London some years before the volcano hit and would not know that my memory of Montserrat which was frozen in time in my mind, would foreshadow freezing in time in reality of a large swathe of the island. How was I to know we would have our own Vesuvius, though we were not thankful for that honour. Reading the sobering experience of the event in my father's book, *Musically and Culturally Montserratian*, and hearing other first-hand stories from family, I pondered Montserrat before and after the volcanic eruption, and I lived through the devastating drama of it as they relived it. My father, Jahdiel's grandpa, was there. In his book, he says that 'a quiet panic began to spread across the island.' The spread of lava was cruelly no respecter of persons. There can be equality in devastation. Sometimes.

And so radical change and adapting must be a part of me, must it not? An enhanced version of all humans' ability to adapt, mould, move on. As I reflect on that seismic shift, I imagine how, much like a volcanic eruption, Jahdiel's arrival reshaped everything.

Ah, the sweet ignorance of that First World, laying in the bath for ages, soaking just because you can. Using the bathroom with the door firmly closed or, dare I say, going one step further and locking it. Privacy, sweet privacy.

Two Worlds

Having a nap because you can. Sauntering off to breakfast, brunch, lunch at a café at any time o'clock. Doing what you want, when you want. Those little pleasures would become lost treasures.

Should I try to cling to the world I knew? How long before acceptance would set in? White flag: I surrender. The high heels give way to kitten heels, give way to trainers and flats. Jahdiel, with his big personality, announced, 'I am here, and there are things that cannot be here. Or certainly cannot be here in the same way.'

The NCT classes and other baby groups, Before Baby, sought to give a tantalising view of that other world. They sought to prepare us as best they could. All great, in theory. There was only so much preparation that could have been done. The wry smile on the NCT practitioner's face conveyed volumes, which I know now was trying to convey that the emotional, mental and psychological preparation we had to figure out for ourselves. In so many respects, learning on the job. Having continuous development, accumulating those CPD points.

But all that is part of what made it exciting when I transitioned, as I had to, to the other world, not knowing that many moments were funny because I just did not see them coming. It was a new season of life you just had to embrace otherwise you would miss it. Otherwise, that new season would embrace you and mould you as it will. It was far better to try—and sometimes fail—to be in the driving seat for that particular journey. So, for better or for worse, for richer or for poorer, in sickness and in health, I moved on to that other world, but you know what? It was a different kind of better. Yes, I, too, was happy to be there.

The Birth

I knew you before I formed you in your mother's womb. Before you were born I set you apart and appointed you as my prophet to the nations.
– Jeremiah 1:5 NLT

'WE'RE PREGNANT!' That is often how it was presented to us. There are often twin smiles on the faces of the expecting mother and expecting father, although the statement invariably comes from the expecting father. The sentiment is admirable, conveying as it does the impression that they are in it together. I never partook in the 'we' as, from my viewpoint, the hard work of that part of our adventure did not sit with me. 'We're pregnant' also seemed a bit too New Age for me.

So, with the birth itself, my role was as the supportive player and I grabbed that baton and sprinted. I was, though, very keen that the world at large be considerate of Josi's impending motherhood. Some of my views were firmly based in first-time-father thinking, or frankly, maybe as simple as my nerves; those, I could amend. Some of my views were unshakeable, whatever the contrary arguments and differing views may be. That all sounds fairly scary, even as I read back to myself what I have just written, but again, the idea of being responsible for an actual human being, having a key role in shaping and developing that human being, was rightly fairly daunting stuff.

We sat in the doctor's office for one of the check-ups. Was there always so much baby stuff in doctors' offices? I do not recall seeing any of it before the existence of baby. Okay, I tell myself, focus on the discussion in the room as the doctor shares information with Josi, rather than on which anatomical part the picture on the wall is supposed to represent. There is an opening in the conversation, and I raise the burning issue that has been on my mind for some time.

'There should be, I opine, much care with maternal movement until the baby beds in properly into the womb. Is that not the case?' Really meant to be a statement of fact rather than a question.

The Birth

Well, it is not put in this way. It goes more like: 'Doctor, maybe my wife should not be jumping around praising during church while pregnant.' Perhaps it is time for quieter contemplation. Should there not be complete calm when listening out for that still small voice?

That was a tumbleweed moment as the doctor looked at me as though she seriously questioned whether I had indeed benefitted from the British education system, let alone Oxford University. There was another moment during which she seemed to be looking for a telltale sign that this was some kind of dad joke. The moment passed, and she quickly reined in her facial expressions and patiently explained to me that I need not worry about the baby needing to be embedded.

Clearly, Doctor, you do not know me, you Embodiment of All Things Maternity. I would ask whatever I needed to. This was not about me. There were more areas of clarification required, and I would pursue them.

For Josi, pregnancy yoga seemed invaluable. The majority of the classes she took were just for expectant mothers. Mother and baby bonding sessions. I imagined the mothers at different stages of pregnancy at those meetings, comparing bumps and wondering how far along each of them was, wearing different types of maternity wear in colours the full spectrum of the rainbow. Some wore 'baby on board' badges, which others think unnecessary as it stated the obvious. Others wondered whether they should get such badges after all and made tentative enquiries as to the ideal place to purchase them.

I imagined an aura of calm in a room that demanded calm, with a practitioner who embodied calmness, not like school classes but immersive experiences. 'Childbirth is completely natural,' the practitioner, I imagined, would not need to say. The very air would let that idea seep into the mothers by osmosis. They would emerge enlightened. They would know why other mothers who have experienced pregnancy yoga had that knowing smile on their faces. The mothers would now just know. I imagined a secret society such that when they were out in the world and saw each other, they gave a knowing nod, a minimal nod that could, perhaps, be imagined if they each did not know what to look out for.

Whatever happened during pregnancy yoga, it helped enormously. I basked in the indirectly reflected rays of peace and contentment. It was a contentment that even though I did not know it, I knew someone who knew it.

So, you can imagine the feeling when the pregnancy yoga practitioner allowed—dare I say, permitted—fathers and partners to attend the inner sanctum of these classes for one session. I am sure everyone would grab the opportunity, much like Charlie going to the Chocolate Factory. It was an opportunity to see the source of all the practice gyrating at

The Birth

home, which, although music was playing, was not, in fact, a new form of dance as of yet undiscovered.

It was in an upper room, pleasantly devoid of unnecessary distractions. The teacher practitioner did, indeed, have a knowing smile. We all came into the yoga room with trepidation, or maybe I was just projecting. For all I knew, the partners had more experience with yoga than the women. For all I knew, the downward dog and manifestation of all such animal poses were second nature to the partners accompanying the women. Again, perhaps much like Charlie, unused to sweet indulgence, when, clearly, some of the other kids at the Chocolate Factory were far too familiar with both sweets and indulgence.

Some wanted to just get in, get it done and get out. Some embraced it. Others had clearly been given secret notes beforehand, so they were familiar with what was about to happen. I would have called it cheating in another context, but in this case, I am kicking myself that I did not try to source the same notes beforehand. It seems to me, as I look back, that pregnancy yoga was one of the best ways to prepare for the big day.

The NCT classes Josi and I attended together were, in many ways, a great part of the preparation for baby. The course leader suggested we have a birthing plan detailing the kind of birth we wanted. It was a bit like picking a meal in a restaurant. Hmmm... that one looks appetising. Can we have these two options but just a taster of that option? No, that option was never in the running and can be put aside, thank you very much. It all seemed so simple when committed to paper in black and white.

The birthing plan, recommended by the NCT practitioner, was almost as detailed as our wedding schedule. Of course, the spelling and grammar were checked for correctness, perhaps convincing myself that the smoothness of the prose would echo the smoothness of the birthing process. Whatever reassured, frankly. Our preparation did not extend to laminating the birthing plan, although I came close to doing so, but it did cover all eventualities. Bags packed? Check. Notifying family and friends? Check. Reconnaissance of the hospital? Check. Routes to the hospital including in the event of road works? Check. In all the thorough preparation, I forgot to ask the baby—no confirmed name at this time, being unaware of the gender—to brush up on the birthing plan before making an appearance. The baby decided to stick to the spirit of the plan if not the detail, which is good enough for legal interpretation of statutes, so good enough for us.

All was more or less in place by the time we got to the hospital for the birth.

***

The Birth

We had music in the midwife-led unit, which helped me, as well as Josi. There was a whole playlist of gospel music meant to help ease the process: calming, beautiful. The birthing pool was nearby in case it was needed. It was like being in a hotel. Almost.

The labour ward had its own kind of music-babies crying from all directions, accompanied by the stark presence of clinical instruments, there for function and nothing more.

My sister, who was looking forward to being Aunty Dawn, was with us at the hospital in the waiting room. To this day, I do not know who was keener to see the little one, me or her.

And then he arrived. He was there. Pause. Pause. Pause. It was a moment that, even now, many years later, brings tears to the eye. The wonder of it all. Any challenges in the build-up to being in that space and that time forgotten. Any future challenges we may encounter as we continued the journey were unknown. There was just the here and now.

That moment is one of those go-to memories that wipes away all nonsense that might be happening in life, any challenges that work and life might bring. It was that cherished moment in time that you wanted to bottle, but not sell, as it belonged only to the two of you and the little one.

The nurses were forgotten; they stepped back, fully conscious that the moment was not for them. Pause. Pause. Pause.

Josi's Reflections

TWO DEAR FRIENDS SENT ME THE SAME BOOK WHILE I WAS PREGNANT. It was about supernatural childbirth. It proclaimed that God did not intend pain during childbirth, which I grabbed on to like the life raft it was. No doubt the book was divine intervention and absolutely necessary because fearful excitement was neither a concoction nor a state of being in which I could remain. Maybe I did not know my own strength, but my fear and trepidation decreased with each turning of the page. It helped manage the narratives that spoke only of screaming, screaming, screaming!

To go from that place to actually enjoying carrying my baby had to have been a miracle. I was greatly helped in that journey by pregnancy yoga. We were a secret society, we pregnancy yoga mothers, an exclusive club open to baby and me, all of us going through the same thing. There was no feeling of being uncomfortable. We were in the same boat, paddling together. There was no need to explain our bodies

The Birth

nor feel as if we stood out in the crowd. We all had a baby on board, so only baby-not-on-board badges were required. I did not need to be the spokeswoman for all pregnant women everywhere, nor did I need to be analysed as to whether motherhood sat well with me. There was no need for the non-pregnant people in the world to accommodate me or for me to be accommodated.

I was, at last, with my pregnancy yoga allies, no longer a minority.

And so, I enjoyed putting on my trainers and going to the classes. There, I was prepared physically and mentally. There, I could put aside, for a moment, so many things whether or not they seemed of importance, like the quandary of buying maternity clothes. Should I buy maternity clothes that still made me feel human, or did I buy so-called normal clothes, just in bigger sizes? There, I could breathe and learn how to breathe. There, I learnt that it was baby and me working in tandem. I was better prepared for what was to come.

With the spiritual guidance of that book and the practical guidance of pregnancy yoga, I was ready when the time came- helped by the two midwives, both named Hannah, who supported me at the hospital. How fitting, how right, that their namesake was an amazing woman from the Bible? Confirmation. And so I could let slide the poking and prodding during ante-natal experiences. I could reclaim the pride and dignity I thought were lost.

As the music played in the midwife-led room, as Edward and I did our own dance, as Aunty Dawn was, no doubt, pacing in the waiting room, in reality, or in her head or both, I realise, looking back, how beautiful it was and how natural it all felt.

Everyone was waiting for him. I felt the expectation of family from all around the world like a physical thing. The biological family, the church family, the 'friends family' — I felt their collective held-in breath. And then he arrived a week early because he, too, could not wait for all of us to meet.

Where's The Manual?

Train up a child in the way he should go: And when he is old, he will not depart from it.
– Proverbs 22:6 KJV

OUT OF THE HOSPITAL, IT WAS TIME TO GET STUCK IN. The health visitor could only do so much. Babies do not come with manuals – how could each individual baby fit in with a set pro forma? No one size fit all. You had to follow your instincts, do what came naturally. What did your parents and grandparents do with you? You will realise when he –

Stop, stop, stop! Yes, they do come with manuals. Sandwiched between the other books on the shelf and the internet, complementing the huge amount of information from ante-natal classes, fighting the good fight against the whole body of knowledge from our Caribbean families. There was a manual. We bought it and intended to use it. Sorry. Dr Caroline Fertleman and Simone Cave, we salute you for your book *Your Baby Week by Week*.

Well-intentioned family—who may or may not have been right—gave some well-intentioned advice. Looking back now, of course, we knew those family members, whose names shall not be mentioned, were often right, but gloating is unbecoming. There is no need to add to any list of I-told-you-sos. Give us a break. We are first-time parents. 'If you don't hear, you'll feel', the phrase often bandied around. Well, sometimes you really did need to feel before you could hear.

Grandma, Josi's mother, was very used to our references to The Book, apparently. Upon visiting her on one occasion, there were two other aunties at her home. One of the aunts made an observation, which was a polite way of saying she kissed her teeth and told us what we were doing wrong at that moment with Jahdiel.

Grandma looked to the well-intentioned family member bestowing the advice and said dismissively, 'Nah, they're following The Book.' Grandma deliberately did not look at Josi or me.

Ouch. I did not realise we had referenced The Book so much in her presence. I looked across to Josi, saying nothing. She looked back at me, joining me in my silence, although her silence clearly wanted to say something. Decision made, she let the comment slide.

Your Baby Week by Week was indeed a well-thumbed, heavily annotated, constant friend. The authors knew their stuff and, even more importantly, knew how to tell it to us. Yep, we knew about the issue raised by the aunt from a specific paragraph on a specific page. Thank you. The more we got various pieces of advice, sometimes conflicting, from various family members, the more it drove us into The Book's loving arms.

You know the end of the story, of course. The Book helped enormously but could not replace the instinctive knowledge of the family, gained from generations of parents' decades of trial and error, like home remedies from back in the Caribbean, imported sometimes, with slight changes. Various plants are often used to deal with aches and ailments in Saint Lucia. Before knowledge of the chemistry behind it, those generations knew which leaf would help with which complaint. In the same way, the vast body of knowledge from family and friends from Saint Lucia and Montserrat helped in child raising without always knowing the reasoning behind it.

That is not to say that the many internet searches did not have their place within reason. There was some scary stuff out there. A deluge of information on every subject you wanted to know about and some subjects you never knew you did not want to know about. Finding reliable sources among the barrage that hit you. And even in the reliable sources, finding the relevant information. The challenge is in taking the information and making judgement calls upon reflection and in the moment when necessary. Sometimes making in the moment decisions when caring for Jahdiel required shutting out the information noise and finding that still small voice. Trusting yourself; dare I say, your instincts?

This was all great in theory. I held my precious, fragile being (PFB) in those first few weeks and months of birth, so concerned about breaking him and causing him stress that I would put the stress and tension into the rest of my body to ensure there was absolutely no tension in the arms that cradled PFB. That arm was the epicentre, immovable. The rest of my body over-compensated for the limb out of use. Feet were used for arms to get this item or pick up that item from the floor. The tone of the demands to others to help with X, Y or Z were said so baby soft it belied the fact they were, in fact, demands. I only slowly and incrementally realised that the fragility was more with me than PFB.

We learned the meaning of different cries when there was meaning. Sometimes realising or wondering whether, perhaps, there was just no translation for that cry. Perhaps PFB just wanted to cry.

Was that, unsatisfactory as it is, the answer?

Where's The Manual

Ah, the crying. Pause. Release the excess air from your mouth that you did not realise you had. They say it affects mothers and fathers differently. Sure, there were times when one of us could bear the cry better than the other, but frankly, you would have to be a stone if you were not affected by the cry in some way. PFB could hit notes you would struggle to find on the piano. As he climbed the octaves, you knew the cry did not sit well with your state of insufficient sleep. You thought it could not go on any further or any longer. Then he went higher.

Like a detective, we sought to establish what the cry was for. I imagined myself as Hercule Poirot (as played by the late Sir Peter Ustinov, of course), trying to impartially examine the facts. He had been fed; okay. He was not wet; fine. All clothes and items that touched his skin were made out of the softest materials known to man, crafted by artists who devoted their lives to making such things. It was not caused by A or Z—could it be colic? That seemed to fit as a running hypothesis.

'Colic? I've never heard of colic. The child has wind!' a seasoned family friend told us with incredulity.

'Ti manmay-la ni van' as we would say in Kweyol, in Saint Lucia.

Whatever you called it, in whatever language, it seemed to have affected him badly. The general practitioner gave us baby Gaviscon, Aptimil and Pepti to give to him together.

The GP was, of course, trying to be helpful to parents who were past their tether and needed urgent assistance. She was the expert, and we trusted her to fix all ills.

That night, after following that advice, the crying took on a whole new level. At that time, we did not know the wise adage of trying one thing at a time to see what would have an effect. Another GP helped redirect us to the right path.

I think it was that episode that really got me to do my pre-GP visit research before seeing what the medics said. It was a delicate balance of not allowing a little knowledge to make me think I knew it all. Not thinking I, myself, could diagnose and prognose as there, too, lay danger. Of course, it could not replace a real life, sitting-in-front-of-you-breathing-in-your-concern doctor, but it sure could put context into what we were told and brush away the cobwebs of ignorance. It was learning the language of illness and disease, knowing what the particular acronyms used by the medics meant, to have the vocabulary to describe what we saw impacting our little one, to know what information and descriptions might help the medic, to know, when we gave the much-needed history, that it was full and relevant.

Maybe the crying wasn't due to colic we then thought. Maybe it was due to his dry skin or a rash. For that, the paediatrician at the hospital suggested some proper moisturising. Yes, the paediatrician from the hospital because sometimes, the cause and prognosis were not apparent to us. Sometimes, it was not clear to the GP either. Indeed, sometimes the best medical advice from the GP was to go to A&E. If it was the weekend, and the GP office was closed, we would have to take him to the hospital, because the issue seemed to us acute and could not wait.

Sometimes, including for those reasons, Accident & Emergency was the way to go, so we went to Children's Accident & Emergency, the land we discovered After Child. When we were at home, if the issue was not resolved to our satisfaction, we would have to go back to Children's A&E.

In all of the conversations about baby before the birth, from multiple sources, welcome or not, they did not tell us about such trips to Children's A&E. I did not even know such a place existed. You went past the main — and I now know, adult — Accident & Emergency until you got to a magical place that had colour, character, tired toddlers and toys. Bright colours assaulted the senses. The blue fish stuck on the wall swam towards the whale-shaped clock. The seahorse mirror looked to be speaking to the crab mirror, the things they must reflect.

Children's programmes were playing on the flat screen television on the wall and play stations with an assortment of toys were dotted around the room. You might forget you were in a hospital but for the posters about measles and polio.

Sometimes It's Funny

I thought the Pied Piper of Hamlin coerced the children into the mountains when the reality was they all came here, to the Children's A&E. The crying babies were accepted by the parents and carers who knew such things happened. You did not feel guilty bringing out your snacks and beverages there; you almost felt obliged to do so since little Johnny needed a snack.

The medical staff looked friendlier. The triage nurses honed the skill of child encouragement into an art form. The mission was to take their temperatures by any means possible, be it with a funny face, silly words, or colourful props.

The pre-birth baby orators and town criers did not tell us about children vomiting again and again. They did not tell us about the times we would feel like we were going crazy because our child would cry (again), that he would be fed, watered, in clean nappy, in clean clothes and in a room that was thermometer-checked for optimal temperature, while still crying. That there were musical notes, known to neither man nor animal, that the little one could access when crying and from which he made music no one wanted to buy.

'Hey, Joanne,' I greeted the receptionist at Children's A&E.

'Hey, Edward—back again so soon?'

'Well, you know, Joanne, the doctors know best. How are Carl and little Vanessa?' It was only polite to ask about the people you felt you knew so well.

'Yeah, Carl still wants to do football, and Vanessa won that competition. You were right, Edward.'

Okay, no such exchange actually took place, but it might as well have done for the number of times we had to pitch up at Children's A&E. Or maybe, like the time spent hearing the cry, the number of times we visited in our minds was much less than the actual number of times in the logbook. The reality of going to A&E anyway was there was always different staff. Frankly, at the time of visiting, remembering names was not uppermost in the mind. We were there for an accident or an emergency. We were not there to take roll call of the various members of staff. We wanted to be dealt with, now. The irony was that the hours spent waiting to be seen by Specialist A or Specialist B sometimes belied that it was, in fact, a place to deal with emergencies. As the hours ticked by and exhaustion increased, it did not occur to me to write down the names of the medic who triaged us, the nurse who came to take vitals or the paediatrician who eventually saw us. We were often in a haze of concern for Jahdiel, with our increasing hunger fighting our increasing frustration.

In all the conversations that people had with us before the birth, the idea of these trips to A&E did not feature. They were silent about that reality.

While well-meaning, they did not tell us about the seemingly never-ending ailments, but The Book helped, in part, to prepare us. Contrary to what you should do with a novel, I jumped forward in The Book to see what we could expect, to see if there were any cliffhangers for which I needed to prepare, to see how that part of the story ended. I needed to know, as Jahdiel seemed to be off from nursery more than he was there. It seemed that we were paying for the privilege of his staying at home. It seemed to me that if a cricket sneezed in Australia, Jahdiel would catch its cold in London.

It was about then that we properly realised, having been through all of that and more, why they did not tell us about those things. Firstly, they did not want to frighten us from having children. The anonymous 'they' gave snippets of child-related issues while I wallowed in ignorance in Before Child world. I listened with half an ear, keeping the other half on anything else. It was interesting but not of direct relevance to me at the time. Or I overheard snippets of stories about crying, vomiting, injections, and so on from stories shared to the room at large. Like small talk, it was entertaining at the time, but it did not really penetrate the lower levels of brain engagement.

Where's The Manual

There were no sit-down conversations about the minutiae of having babies. With hindsight, I am sure friends, relatives and colleagues with children monitored my eyes to see how much information could safely be imparted before a degree of fear crept into the eyes of the listener: me. Searching for that sliver of fear that indicated I might swear off children forever more if they gave me too much information.

So, the snippets of the gory details invariably ended with, 'But I would never change it for the world!' spoken with such force in an attempt—sometimes thinly veiled—to undo any suggestion that having little Johnny was not the best thing ever.

They wanted me to join their world, so even during the pregnancy, the snippets still came with a careful eye-watching to see how much they could share the reality.

Secondly, they thought—rightly—that I would not quite understand unless I had gone through it myself. As if, like children, however much we were told about fire, we did not quite get it until we felt the heat ourselves. Or maybe it was more like that delicious-looking mango dangling from the mango tree, ripening before our very eyes. However much we might have salivated imagining the juiciness, however much we were told of the taste, we could not know it for ourselves without partaking: the thread of the mango getting in your teeth, the rotten bit on the side. Fire or mango—which suits you best, Jahdiel? Fire mango; is that a thing?

Sometimes It's Funny

Thirdly, the well-meaning friends and family forget. The mind can be a wonderful thing. It was like the intensity of late nights spent revising for finals at university falling away from the mind: a protective mechanism. Surely, it was the same thing with the minute-by-minute minutiae of raising a baby. For example, it is only when I sharply focus that I remember the drama of changing Jahdiel when we were on our way to get his first Start Rite shoes, that delicate balance of knowing what time we should leave the house so we would be well-placed when he needed food, that semi-panic of whether we would find a space to feed Jahdiel at the due time. It was the firm belief that if feeding came a minute later than the due time, dire consequences would follow, the repercussions of which would be felt by him all the way to his choosing the wrong woman to be his wife; we did not want to bear that responsibility.

The irony was that there was a manual, but it is only created after the event. Looking back, I can now say what happened, what we did and what we should have done. Sometimes, these answers were the same thing, sometimes not. Yes, it would have been very helpful if we could have gone back in time. This was probably why it was often said that parents are more relaxed with baby number two and those who came after. Maybe they were more informed and less tense. Even the information and knowledge gained by raising baby number one was seemingly forgotten. In reality,

Where's The Manual

it becomes a part of our muscle memory. We become a manual of sorts. Or, at least, the manual for Jahdiel, which was really as far as we could go. Some chapters would be relevant for all; many would be personal to him.

But there was another overarching manual in another book. I mention this manual last, although, in reality, it came first and was always available to us, even when I did not think it was such. It provided guidance, comfort, instruction and lessons, even those that were hard to swallow or fully understand in the moment. It contained the snippets we show to you in quotations after each chapter's name. It is not ours to give but for you all to have if you want it. It is, of course, the Bible. And so faith in God, informing faith in manuals, helped guide us through when we knew it as such and even when we did not realise that our Guide was always there.

Josi's Reflections

WE DID SEARCH FOR OTHER MANUALS. Beyond The Book, beyond any print, to the pages of chapters written in memory. The accumulated learning and wisdom of all those who had gone before us, family and friends.

Those who had been on this journey survived and, dare I say, even thrived.

The search for guidance led me to a weaning class recommended by the NCT practitioner. I sat again among so many who did not look like me, save the person looking back at me from the mirror across the room. But I was misled by experience, spoiled by the memories of baby yoga and the comforting feeling that we mothers are in this together.

As we sat in a room within a spacious semi-detached home with its very many rooms, the conversation turned to the appropriate age at which to start weaning. United, as I believed we were in our motherhood, I felt empowered to share how, in some Caribbean and African cultures, we introduced solids earlier, including very lightly made porridges, sometimes adding milk to thicken it.

The course trainer clipped, 'I don't know about that. We, in the U.K., don't start to wean until six months,' then swiftly moved on.

I said nothing, and neither did anyone else. That nothing sat in a sliver of uncomfortable silence.

In two short sentences, the trainer had created a gulf between me and all of them. She no doubt imagined me recently arrived here, ignorant of the norms of the motherland about which I clearly needed to be enlightened. I looked at the reflection in the mirror again and wished we could swap places.

I then stared at the reflection of the course trainer in that mirror, not trusting myself to face the real woman. How dare you seek to invalidate my lived experiences? How dare you seek to belittle the wisdom built on generations of people and caressed under the nourishing heat of my island with your careless words, spat out like venom?

I shut up and shut down, reminded again that I was an island in a sea of those who did not look like me. In a general way, I was aware that I was the sole flag, but I was not aware that I was supposed to be responsible for flying that flag.

The session ended, and I left, never to return. It was a hard lesson on those memory pages that I am tempted to discard, but this, too, was a part of learning, the manuals, so it must be kept for fear of losing the lesson.

It was experiences like this that caused a heavier reliance on The Book. Within its well-written prose, it made no judgement. It gave no cultural slight recklessly presented, as any such thing would have been ruthlessly edited away. But just like Edward's detailed birthing plan document, no one thought to tell Jahdiel that he needed to read The Book, far less to follow it. No one told him that he could not behave in that particular way because that was in Chapter 5, and we were still in Chapter 3. He decided, in so many ways, to go off-script. There was no Jahdiel-specific chapter or even footnote to let me know that sometimes, he just wanted his voice heard because his voice was and would be a big part of who he was. There was no appendix that spoke of a toddler who would use those same vocal cords in song after song. Nor, as granddad would say, that he was simply exercising his right to protest.

So, in the moment, we asked ourselves what the neighbours might make of the crying. I think of those friends who gave tales of their babies who hardly cried—was that the norm? We, therefore, prepared speeches for those same neighbours when they knocked on our door—as they surely would—to ask, 'Is he all right?' That they did not knock, that they did not ask, must have meant they had already made their judgement, which was even more damning. In a world that contained only me, Edward, Jahdiel and the crying, which was surely a fourth, uninvited person who had stayed far too long, all sense of perspective was gone.

The weight of the information and learning from all quarters did not warn me about the optimum way of preserving cream carpets during potty training or when its friend, diarrhoea, made an appearance! So, I ran behind him with the wipes and disinfectant, which he thought was a game. I am not playing, Jahdiel. I am not amused.

I cast my mind back to Edward and me at the carpet shop when I looked at the darker colours with disdain, having walked past the wooden flooring store without pausing.

In those Before Child days, only a cream carpet with its warmth and light fit my colour scheme for our home.

The information got to be too much at times and it was conflicting. Do not bathe the baby after delivery versus bathe the child — don't you know where we are from Josi? Do not use anything on his skin as he has natural oils versus are you losing sense, Josi? You have to use shea butter, Vaseline and coconut oil now! Do not start weaning too early versus give the child Cream of Wheat, arrowroot or baby rice — have you forgotten what we did back home?

They all meant well, but sometimes, I turned down their volume or put them on mute. I stepped back, even when there seemed no time to step back, and like a sieve, shook all of that information through the lens of my child. I allowed myself time to see what remained for him, trusting in Him.

And so, amidst all the helpful and not-so-helpful musings of others and the thoughts that might have come from my own fallible understanding, I tried to stay strong in that overarching manual, the Bible, as it inspired and encouraged throughout our journey of parenthood. In particular, it was absolutely necessary on those days when we felt completely out of our depth. There was a constant reminder in the powerful words of Proverbs 3:5-6 KJV, sometimes voiced through others: 'Trust in the Lord with all thine heart; And lean not unto thine own understanding. In all thy ways acknowledge him, And he shall direct thy paths.'

Kiss at the Bars and All Those Ahhh Moments

Out of the mouth of babes and sucklings hast thou ordained strength.
– Psalm 8:2 KJV

IT WAS WHEN I TOOK MY HEAD OUT OF THE BOOKS AND RESEARCH THAT I BEGAN TO PROPERLY APPRECIATE THE WONDER OF THAT PRECIOUS, FRAGILE BEING. When we were getting married, someone wisely told us to take a moment during the day for just the two of us to enjoy the moment. Among the rushing around to make sure everyone else had a good time, those who host and organise parties and celebrations could forget to eat, forget to dance, forget to breathe. When balancing work and home, breathing could seem secondary, but it was so important. Otherwise, such beautiful moments would just be missed or enjoyed long after the event; do not miss them.

Who could forget the first time they felt warm baby urine on their face, the drops threatening to make their way into their mouth? It was an ahhh moment, but only after looking back. Before it happened to me for the first time, after so many months of nappy changes, my confidence was again high thinking that I was an expert at changing nappies. I thought that aspect of parenting had been firmly ticked and focus could be given to other aspects of parenting. I remember that Jahdiel was doing his usual half-wriggling on the changing mat. I was humming a ditty to myself that popped into my head, a song that probably only half existed. No need, therefore, I thought, to cover the offending orifice while I was changing the nappy, as I would be super-fast. The spray, when it came, was a surprise, and for precious milliseconds, I was in shock and forgot to react in self-preservation. I choose to remove from my memory whether urine actually mixed with saliva as my mouth opened in a slow exclamation of 'Noooooo!',

There are sometimes precious, sweet moments which were both precious and sweet at the time. This was the other kind. That category about which the descriptors 'precious' and 'sweet' only attached with time. A long time.

Kiss at the Bars and All Those Ahhh Moments

We got used to stuff on our hands from every one of the baby's bodily orifices—let us call it *stuff and* let us say that it just gets on your hands. Acknowledge it. Wipe it. Move on. These, too, were moments made precious only with time.

With Jahdiel, each day was something new. Or so it seemed. Yet another point 'they' would make to me in Before World. Yet another occasion for me to sniff, smile politely and kiss my teeth in my head. How annoyingly right that amorphous 'they' were again.

One of the most exquisite new things was the first steps. Aunty Dawn came over to our house for one of her routine visits. She was determined that she would not be a stranger to Jahdiel, that she would be firmly fixed in his growing mind as 'AUNTY DAWN', with all letters capitalised. That she would be highly significant to him was not even a battle, because if it were, she would win. She would get far too gleeful and smug when, in time, we video phoned her, and Jahdiel yelled, 'AUNTY DAWN,' his tone clearly capitalising each letter.

So, this was one of her visits building to the glee-smug video calls that would come. It was early evening in early winter. Jahdiel's first birthday was approaching in a matter of weeks. The plans were already in place. The theme was winter because that was when it was. We banished from our minds—not wholly successfully—the messages from the NCT parents group chat about little Johnny or little Janey having made their first steps, when Jahdiel had not yet done so. A message from the NCT classes played like a mantra in my head: 'Each child progresses at their own pace. Each child progresses at their own pace. Each child—' Yep, I got the point. Maybe I should put the group chat notifications on silent. Sometimes, I had to.

I kept an eye on Jahdiel as I gave Aunty Dawn an update on all the developments with baby since her visit the week before. We formed a protective triangle around him in the hallway with its wooden flooring. Although we were long past the fear of him crossing the threshold from the carpeted floor of the living room to the heart-stopping danger of the wooden flooring, we were not past constant vigilance around him.

I manned the door to the living room, the easy job. If Jahdiel reversed back into the living room with the carpet's warm embrace, it would not be a bad thing.

Josi womaned the bottom of the stairs, multi-tasking and juggling the front door. It was firmly shut and locked, but who knew what new and unforeseen danger might arise from that quarter at a moment's notice.

Aunty Dawn womaned the door to the kitchen with its obvious dangers. Therein lay the obvious cupboards, sharp edges and so forth, but of much more concern, the tiled flooring, a creature to which Jahdiel had yet to be exposed.

Kiss at the Bars and All Those Ahhh Moments

Then it happened: Jahdiel put both hands on the floor, pushed his bottom up so that his arms were straight and so were his legs, then he pushed himself up onto his feet. I grabbed Josi. She grabbed me. We stared mesmerised, not wanting to move a muscle, neither saying nor wanting to say a word.

I moved only my eyes to dare a glimpse across at Aunty Dawn, who I was sure was blinking far too loudly. A glimpse was all I could spare. By willpower alone, I gave Jahdiel a little push. His little right foot raised achingly slowly a baby metre in the air (a few centimetres, if that) and crashed to the floor a baby metre forward (again, centimetres if that).

None of us breathed. Well, I could not speak for the other two, but I knew that if it went on for too much longer, I risked struggling for a breath.

Jahdiel's little left foot raised precariously into the air and crashed down to the floor. His right foot dared to go for an encore. It was all too much. His well-nappied bottom met the floor and decided that it was the better option than the complexity of walking. Job done for now.

The elation was too much. Josi and I jumped up and down, hugging, laughing, shouting. The joy was exquisite. No baby ever walked so confidently; I was sure. In the moment, we knew there had never been, nor would there ever be, anything so wonderful. This meant the world would be his oyster. Another milestone was smashed. We felt like we could have held the birthday party then and there rather than wait, to celebrate the never-before-seen event.

Aunty Dawn tried to be the calm one, but her smile betrayed the for-goodness-sake-people look on her face. She did not jump and hug, though I suspect it would be a moment that replayed in her mind and made her smile on her way home.

Fast forward to getting Jahdiel's first shoes. Take a moment to pause and reflect on the world of fitting specialised shoes, half-sizes, names known to the industry that are alien to the uninitiated. Not just length but also the width of the shoe adds an exponential number to the amount of shoe permutations. It was another baby thing.

I checked in with Grandmama, my mother, to see what that was like for me as a young child growing up in Saint Lucia in the 1980s. We did not have the constant upgrading of shoes every few months or less as my feet grew bigger. I am sure I had shoes to grow into, not shoes to grow out of.

'Just push socks in the end,' the adults from my youth would have said.

'He'll grow into it'.

I wiggle my toes, sure my feet have not ended up irreversibly traumatised from the lack of a constant change of shoes, each one incrementally larger than the last, though this seemed a must with Jahdiel.

Kiss at the Bars and All Those Ahhh Moments

It was, therefore, with a sniff and an upturned nose, that we gathered the paraphernalia that always went with going out with a baby as we prepared to visit the shoe shop for the first time. Jahdiel's eyes lit up at the exciting new things he saw whilst we were on the bus. We looked with fresh eyes at the previously mundane experience of being on the bus, starting to see it from his perspective. The annoying dog, which was clearly too large to be allowed on a bus, turned into a shaggy, mythical creature whose lolling tongue was an exciting shade of red. The crush of the crowd became baby millions of people who were not Mama and Papa. The pressing of that button was now longingly linked to a bell and magically made the bus stop.

And so, by the time we approached the shoe shop, I was willing to concede, not reluctantly, that this was, indeed, an adventure.

What a joy to see Jahdiel prance around the store in his first Start Rite shoes. I never really understood what prancing was until I saw it. They were electric red, and we wondered how the colour will fit in with the rest of his clothes. They wouldn't, but who cared? They were statement shoes. They shouted, 'These are my first pair of shoes. Look at them. Look at me!' We wondered whether he would stay still long enough to put on the shoes, which was clearly a misplaced concern. He was eager to put them on as he seemed to think the shoes, like wings, were things to help him move faster.

I dashed across the shop floor, not having factored into the equation that the shoes would make him faster on his feet. Looking around, I wondered whether they came in adult sizes so I could keep up with him.

It was only a matter of time before 'He kicked the ball!' was another first that brought a tear to my eye. I was excited as the ball went a baby mile down the lawn, projected there by Jahdiel's expertise. Of course, we knew the exact date the football incident took place; there were photographs of the important key event.

There was also a text sent out to all family and friends with photographic and video evidence to support this. We had to pretend the video sent was the recording of the actual event since when it first happened, the camera was not out and primed. I briefly considered whether there should just be cameras around the house recording at all times so that nothing would be missed.

Uncle Des, in particular, had to be pleased, and he was the first one to whom the video of the event was sent. 'Hey, Des,' I messaged him.

'Hey, Ed. What's up?'

'I'm sending you a video of Jahdiel kicking a football!' I texted to forewarn him about the amazing thing he was about to see. I sent him the full video clip.

Kiss at the Bars and All Those Ahhh Moments

'Nice. I can buy that kit for him now?' I knew he was waiting for the right time to send a football kit to his nephew.

Was that not another defining moment weighed with promise for the future? Did it not represent the many firsts he would achieve in his life? Would each one not eclipse all previous firsts?

'Oh, that's nice,' someone else replied when I mentioned the momentous event, deflating my excitement. That person clearly did not appreciate its import. Sometimes, these things were only important and only carried high significance to us. I kissed my teeth anyway.

Of course, we had photographs of moments such as those, carefully captured video clips from the mighty mobile-always-in-our-pocket just for those moments. They were indelibly etched in our minds as examples of seminal milestones. Clearly, only our child, out of all children in the world, had ever kicked a ball in such a way at such an age. The photographs and video clips were carefully and painstakingly saved in a special virtual photograph album.

It was with these videos that Grandma was able to hear Jahdiel saying words we did not even realise he is saying at the time. As much as we see and hear, there were a whole host of events we took part in but did not realise they were happening at the time.

As his vocabulary built, we realised he was listening and taking it all in, and we were even more careful about what was said around him. We built a body of phrases to replace words of frustration and startlement, like 'Oh, dear!' 'Oh sugar,' and 'Oopsy.' Stock phrases that rapidly became second nature because they were palatable to a baby's and toddler's ears. As children, my parents did not swear in front of us, so I would like to think that and any accidental utterances would sound alien on my tongue. Right up there with trying to sound *street*. So, I am relatively safe in that area. When the pain of a stubbed toe was too much, I was forced to quickly shut my eyes and take a deep breath, as Jahdiel was looking on.

In time, my 'circle of oopsy' became larger, and I was empowered to say to a group of young men on the bus, 'Do you mind? My son's here,' when their language got too colourful. I layered, I hoped, the comment with double delivery: a demand to them; said as a saccharine off-hand comment to Jahdiel's ears. I also directed a warning to a good friend who used expletives like punctuation, that she was on loudspeaker and a certain little person was within earshot. That friend knows who she is.

Who knew the word 'please' could be a weapon? In the mouth of a toddler, it made many an unreasonable request seem so... well... reasonable. It threatened to tip you into the go-on-then-just-this-once camp; go on — have that extra treat. Couple that with those large doe eyes, glistening on demand. What other tactics were marinating in that

Kiss at the Bars and All Those Ahhh Moments

developing brain of his? I would like to think of it as a skill that would bode well for him in the future. Perhaps he would be able to convince others in a powerful way. There I go, thinking again.

Out of so many precious moments, it was the kissing at the bars that ranked high up there in the ahhh-count, for me. This happened when Jahdiel was properly old enough to say goodnight. Josi and I shared the bedtime routine, or we alternated: the bath, reading, the prayers before bed. Before I put him to bed for the last part, he needed to say goodnight to Mama. The stair gate was closed at the top of the stairs as a continuation of the bannister farther along the hallway. Mama was on the other side of the bannister. It was dark but light enough that the white of the bars of the bannister were clear in the darkened hallway.

How did these things, these precious moments start? The best of moments were not manufactured, nor were they doctored. There was no video of that moment. I think it would be spoiled if there were.

Jahdiel walked in his now confident way up to the bars of the bannister, said, 'Kiss,' and kissed Mama through the first gap in the bars. Then, he went to the next gap. 'Kiss,' and the next, 'Kiss,' and the next until there were no gaps left through which to kiss Mama.

Job done, he meandered back to his bedroom, sleepier now that the essential task had been done. So simple, so touching. Our hearts melted. That became a routine. Like many moments, it lasted for only a short season before something else became the routine.

I miss kissing at the bars.

Josi's reflections

MUSIC HAS REALLY BEEN A LARGE PART OF THE PARENTHOOD JOURNEY WITH OUR SON. Edward's good friend Naila bought and sent over a toy Thomas the Tank Engine for Jahdiel from the United States, where she lived. Jahdiel could sit on it, and it played various Thomas-themed baby music. He discovered the button to make the music play without needing to sit on the toy. At that stage, he could finally stand independently.

Pressing the button over and over again for the music to play, he bobbed up and down to the beat. Looking like he was doing squats, he did some mean dancing for minutes on end. There was intent in his dancing. He made an 'uh-uh' sound, mimicking the key beats of the music. We were in hysterics as he did this over and over again, pressing the button, bobbing along, sounding the beats.

We watched him, sometimes dancing with him, most times just smiling away. We were being entertained and

Kiss at the Bars and All Those Ahhh Moments

brought along by his pleasure. This moment was stored in my laughter catalogue. It was easily accessible when the day was cold, and there was too much going on in the world, and I just needed to smile it all away.

Maybe for Jahdiel the important thing was travel and speed. He slid down the stairs from the first to the ground floor at home on his tummy as he was apprehensive about walking down, or maybe he was just enjoying the game of it. He slid down in a star shape, legs at 20 past 8 and arms at 10 minutes past 10. He went at a speed that would later frighten a friend from church when we sent her the video of him bumping along the contours of the stairs.

I reflected that, thankfully, we decided to put thick carpet on the stairs and that his clothing protected him from carpet burn.

He was unsure how to get back up the stairs. Not entirely confident with walking yet, he traversed four mountainous steps on his hands and knees. It was his Everest. He stopped and looked back, knowing he had gone so high, and I think he thought how wonderful a thing that was. He looked up and saw that he was not even halfway there, and he had a long way to go.

I saw his uncertainty about the situation, no longer sure if he wanted to or could keep going up. Tentatively, I asked, 'Um, what will you do now? How will you get down?'

Instinctively, as if there could only be one possible option, he reached out one hand to me or to Edward with the other clutching the bannister, confident we would rescue him. We hoped that confidence would always be there, eroded though it might be as the years passed. When do our children stop seeing us as superheroes who can do no wrong? In that moment, we both smiled, and I scooped him up, much to his giggling delight.

As he grew, he transitioned from the cot to a toddler-sized bed in his own room. It seemed small in his room, but he was very excited by the event. We, too, were very excited about his new milestone. In the moment, we did not know that the bed would be part of the challenge at sleep time now that he was able to exit his sleeping quarters on his own steam, the bars of the cot having vanished. It meant many visits from a little person during many nights, coming into Mama and Papa's room.

We did not know that as we watched him jumping up and down and rolling around, on his bed. He must have been thinking that he was a big boy deserving of a big boy bed. That he wore a toddler sleeping bag with holes for his legs, gave the scene a comic slant. As he ready-steady-go jumped off the bed again and again, all we knew in that room bathed in the light of day was that he was so happy, that it did not take much for such exquisite happiness and that we wanted to continue basking in that space and time.

Kiss at the Bars and All Those Ahhh Moments

It was a happiness that was mirrored in his first experience of snow. We were on our road in front of the house, which was closed off to traffic because of the snow. The freshly fallen snow covered the homes, the vehicles, the road and the trees in a picturesque way. Edward busied himself taking pictures to send to family in Saint Lucia. Children were sledging with makeshift or actual sledges along the road. Snowball fights were getting started in front of a couple of the houses. The neighbours who thought it too cold or treacherous to wander outside gazed out from their windows, smiling in spite of themselves.

There was no need for discussion as the consensus was implied: we had to go outside for Jahdiel to experience this. He was in a full snowsuit with a hat, scarf, gloves and boots. Due to the thickness of the insulation keeping him warm, he not so much walked as wobbled. With two little words from him, 'Stay there,' which was both an instruction to us and to himself, we paid full attention to him as he smiled with glee. Staring up to the sky, captivated by this never-before-experienced event, he giggled as the snow melted on his face, and we celebrated with him.

Yes, the kiss at the bars that Edward described, that precious moment in time that now seems all too short, is right near the top of the list of the ahhh moments. Diamond. But does it battle with a slither of time that I remember, even shorter, which was personified love?

A brief time like a single drop of water in a sea of beautiful memories, when Jahdiel was just barely about to vocalise words, when he was only a few months old. Speaking would put it too high. It was just me and him in the living room, and I was singing to him: 'I love you. I love you.' He picked up the melody and copied the sounds I made. He could barely articulate the words but even then, he had the rhythm of speech. With perfect pitch intonation, he echoed my voice as he sang back 'oo ooo ooo'. My heart melted. It was one of those rare occasions I was immensely pleased to have my mobile telephone with me. It, too, saw the event, recorded it and committed it to memory.

Musical Interlude

Make a joyful noise unto the Lord.
– **Psalm 100:1 KJV**

O come, let us sing unto the Lord: Let us make a joyful noise.
– **Psalm 95:1 KJV**

IT STARTED IN THE WOMB, SINGING TO THE BABY WHILE PREGNANT. He was just 'the baby' at the time, not knowing the gender but just wanting a healthy child. Music was played at home. Whether played softly or blasting out, it was, and it was linked with dancing because the music compelled movement, whether big or small. There was music in the car, music at church with full percussion, organ, piano, violin and keyboard accompaniment. Music, music, music.

Sometimes It's Funny

It was not intentional, I do not think, just a part of the sphere we were and are in.

Maybe, actually, it was before then, and it is also down to genetics. Josi can sing and not just in-the-shower-when-you-are-on-your-own-with-no-one-to-hear-you singing. The tear-inducing, really touches you singing. Grandpa, Josi's father, is Flasha Daley, who played with Arrow — trumpet, guitar… he plays it all. I do not count my out-of-practice oboe or gone-back-to-basics piano playing. There is clearly enough in the genes to ring true. How else to explain Jahdiel's uncanny rhythm and pitch?

One of the most common songs we sang and played was 'So Will I (100 billion x)' from Hillsong. Oh, that song. Many a time when he needed to sleep that song was played. The sheep can stay in the pasture, chewing away whatever it is they chew — who needed to count them? Who needed driving round the block a few times? Who needed to delve into those old-school remedies that have fallen out of favour? Just play the song. Again and again. Play it so much that you not only knew all the words but the notes of every instrument. Play it until you knew all the pauses.

When he was months older, Jahdiel started to recognise the start of the song, and he knew what it meant. The opening notes played and he fussed, knowing what the song foretold, knowing that we were trying to lull him to sleep. But resistance was futile and had to be. We wanted to

Musical Interlude

be careful, though. We did not want to abuse the musical power given to us. It was not just a case of with great power comes great responsibility; it was being conscious of not building an immunity to the precious gift and find it was ineffective when needed.

Music played while driving in the car with him. The songs he liked, he asked to play over and over again. And again. We all sang along. Then, he wanted it again and again until I began to believe I no longer liked that particular song. He knew what he liked, and it only took a few notes of a new song for him to proclaim 'no', meaning that he did not like the song. Otherwise there was the more positive silence, which meant he deemed that the song could continue. Deemed it had enough merit to be heard to the very end, after which a final judgement would be pronounced: 'Again!'

One day, we took Jahdiel to Jackie's home in North London. No special occasion; it was just a visit to see family, although that was always special one way or another. The need for him to interact with his family was important. Family was important. As usual, music played in the car on the way to Jackie's home.

In Jackie's home, there was more music playing. There were toys and entertainment all round for the children. In his usual way, Jahdiel eased into the process of engaging with the family. Time passed. He was just getting used to his cousins, especially Jarrel, who was similar in age to him. He was just starting to warm up and get into the groove of playing with them when it happened: let us park what happened for the moment and give some context.

Unfortunately, Jahdiel does not see his maternal family as often as we would like as they live United Kingdom far (at least one hour) away. The weekdays were taken up with nursery, and Jahdiel was often tired when he came home. Sundays were taken up with church, more or less for the whole day. It fell to precious Saturdays to fight with swimming, birthday parties, shopping or stuff unspecified but seemingly important at the time. So, he visited family but not as often as we would have liked. Then COVID-19 and lockdown added a whole other layer of apologies and we-would-love-to buts.

So, do not blame us parents, family; I hear you kiss your teeth so violently there is the risk of a dentist visit. Do not totally blame us parents; bear all this in mind and draw back your judgement.

So, back to the *it* that happened. Three older cousins walked into the space where Jahdiel and his two younger cousins were playing merrily. The older cousins were between 18 and 35 years, each a force of nature in their own way, each a presence who filled the room. Together, their combined presence filled the room to overflowing.

Musical Interlude

'What, Jahdiel—you don't know your cousin? You're not saying hi?' It begins.

'I blame your parents. If they brought you to see me, you'd know who I am.' This brash approach did not work with him.

'Ah, leave him,' said Cousin Number Two. 'Hey, Jahdiel—you saying hi?' Pause.

'I saw some pictures of you,' Cousin Number Two continued. This encouraging approach did not work either.

Cousin Number Three said nothing. She just looked across at Jahdiel now and then with what was meant to be a smile of camaraderie. Nope. Three strikes.

'He's appropriately suspicious of the world.' That was what a good friend insightfully said of our son. It was far more eloquently said than kissing your teeth and wondering what was wrong with the child.

This is your family, I think. For better or for worse, for richer or for poorer, in sickness and in health, and so on, so you should find an instant connection with them. Surely, there was something on the genetic level that automatically extended and granted such an affinity. Surely?

If a thing like that existed, it had not kicked in yet. Jahdiel drew closer and closer to us until he was sitting on my lap. His eyes remained on them as they had done since the older cousins first entered the room. He said not a word. He looked across the room as though unsure of what to make of the force of nature that disturbed the enthralling game of fire truck.

There was not a word from him as we packed up and walked to the car. We overstayed anyway and had to get home. There was not a word as he got into his car seat and was strapped in.

Then, 'Jesus, I need you. Every moment, I need you,' he sang in a clear, angelic voice. We burst out laughing, then turned our heads covering our mouths trying not to show the laughter. Then, we looked at each other, thinking of the layers involved in that scene.

He went back to his usual chatty self as we sped off home.

On another occasion, two of those same older cousins saw Jahdiel, and he waved to them as we were heading home.

'Ah, look: he's saying hi,' said one cousin.

'No,' the other replied. 'He never says hello. He only says bye to me.'

Hmmm. I did not really know what to say to that. There was singing and dancing on that occasion, too.

Singing is a comfort and a passion for him. Singing first thing in the morning. Singing during the day and in the evening. Grandpa bought him a harmonica. He had a banjo and a guitar and a little piano. He kept rhythmically banging on everything to make us wonder whether he shouldn't have some drums.

Musical Interlude

There is a virtual album filled with clips of him singing whole songs and fragments of songs, banging away to some ditty or another. We wondered whether there was a future for him in music of some kind or another. Meanwhile, wherever it might lead, music was a wonderful all-embracing friend for the three of us as we marched on.

Josi's Reflections

WHERE DID RESPONSIBILITY LIE? Who or what should we thank for music being such a central feature of who Jahdiel is? Was it because of playing the song Aunty Dawn liked during labour: Hillsong's 'Broken Vessels (Amazing Grace)'? I wanted to reframe that word 'labour' anyway, connoting, as it did, oppressive work, a chore. We sought to reframe the experience of childbirth, and music was a key part of that. Had something been written into his DNA because of his exposure to music before he was even born?

Barely able to crawl, he gravitated to the Baby Einstein piano attached to his play mat. Banging away, I'd assumed he was just attracted to the colours, the shapes and the sound. The Book told us about that type of stimulation. I would later read about how music could be important for brain development, but in the moment, I just sang to him as he sang voicelessly back to me. He seemed to really enjoy that.

He went from having a baby microphone to a toddler microphone to what he really wanted: a proper adult microphone. But even during his microphone journey, he used the xylophone stick, a toothbrush and a spoon as microphones. Indeed, anything mike-like. He drummed away on the table using coasters, using books. With Grandpa's harmonica came the xylophone from Aunty Sissy, so that he now had two. He had a guitar — should we buy those drums? Would the same neighbours, whom we imagined holding quiet judgement about Jahdiel's crying, have views about a full set of toddler drums?

Jahdiel was obsessed with music, which, as time passed, refined to include singing. Needing no audience, he was often in a concert for one by one.

I was transported back to my own childhood, with my five- or six-year-old self standing at the top of my grandmother's road in Montserrat, singing at the top of my lungs, hoping that someone at the bottom of the hill would hear. Wanting my voice to project past the mango trees, coconut trees and grape trees that stood to attention by the side of the road. Past the houses tucked away on either side of the road. Past the bamboo house where the lovely Rastafarian family lived. Past the hibiscus and the croton plants that huddled together, shaking with laughter

Musical Interlude

from the wind as though sharing some secret known only to them. Past the goats, who were startled by the sound. Past the cow, who sat lazily on the grass chewing her cud, barely acknowledging my concert as it was something she had seen and heard far too often, turning her head to her calf and a patch of grass which, for her, were far more interesting but letting out an acknowledging *moo* despite herself. Past the veranda in grandmother's house into the living room and into the ears of my grandmother. She paused, she heard, she smiled, and she carried on.

My time capsule paused at our church in Montserrat, reminding me that my young self sang in church, obliged to sing by Uncle Will, pastor of the church, though sometimes, wanting to sing. But let us be crystal clear: all of us young ones had to do something in the church — anything — so wanting to do that thing was a fringe bonus but, frankly, irrelevant to the outcome. My task was to sing, and sing, I did. 'A sunbeam, a sunbeam; Jesus wants me for a sunbeam,' I sang again and again.

It was now Jahdiel's turn to shine.

And so, I never tell Jahdiel to stop singing. Even when he wants to duet with me again and again. Even when I feel too tired to sing, exhausted from being in his world. Exhausted from all the micro-decisions that have to be taken all day because of the force that he is. His singing takes me from a place of low to a place of joy. It was not a choice, just like

Uncle Will's demands. Jahdiel sang you into submission. If you initially wanted to come along for the ride, it was all well and good, but your initial intention was irrelevant. It was where you ended that mattered, which was a stirring of your spirit. Isaiah 61:3 KJV speaks of *the garment of praise for the spirit of heaviness* – how well that fits.

I looked again at a video of Jahdiel when he was one year and ten months young. It has been played so many times that if it was on a compact disc, I suspect it would be overheated and damaged by now!

Jahdiel and I were sitting in my bedroom. I was off camera as he, alone, filled the frame, wearing his 'Best Dude' jumper. The photographs of Edward and me on the walls of the room can just about be made out on screen. Jahdiel was staring into the camera, fiddling with his plaits and singing Bob Marley's 'Three Little Birds' while I sang background vocals. I was often only the supporting act to his main event, but that was all right.

Having sung that song before, I, in a moment of clarity, decided to record it to see if he would do it again. He was still learning to speak, and some of the words were not fully formed, but that only made it all the more cute and powerful for his rendition.

It was undeniably piercing when he sang the words about not worrying and that things would be alright. He

Musical Interlude

warned the viewer/listener when he pointed his little right index finger as he sang, that the message was for us.

My cousin in Antigua told me that she played the video to her clients at one of her counselling sessions. It did what it was intended to do; it lifted their spirits.

Fast forward seven months later. Edward, Jahdiel and I were at his last Health Visitor appointment. We sat in a room filled with instruments of assessment. The scales were on one side, next to a small bed. The sink in the corner welcomed our coming into the room and would wish us well going out, as we had to wash our hands both times. It was well-used as we were coming out of COVID lockdown. The one window helped the light in the room and faced some trees, using nature to give us all privacy. It was nearing the summer, and the cheery green of the leaves and mellow browns of the branches nicely contrasted with the stark white of the walls of the room.

Edward and I sat on chairs facing the Health Visitor, who sat at the table with a clipboard and pen poised, ready to leave the starting blocks and begin the race to the end of the assessment. It indeed felt like a test that, unbeknownst to him, Jahdiel had to take. We were anxious on his behalf; thankfully, he was free of adult anxiety. Would he be assessed as meeting his milestones? Would he get an A in all domains, or would a B or C do? Had we done our homework and revision properly to equip him to go to the next stage?

Jahdiel was weighed, and he was standing next to the table, examining the pack provided by the Health Visitor and, in particular, a book. The Health Visitor scribbled away, a crease forming on her forehead as she concentrated. Edward tried to read her notes upside down to see what grades we'd been given. I wondered, in passing, what her creased forehead meant.

Then, Jahdiel, out of nowhere, started singing in a clear, angelic voice. He sang with a fluidity of words that he did not yet have when he spoke. He sang 'I Prevail', and we all froze.

The Health Visitor's pen stopped one centimetre above the page, the word unfinished, her hand frozen above the page. I suspect she no longer saw the page, and I do not know what flashed across her mind. The song spoke of how God helps you prevail over sickness, prevail over weapons formed against you, prevail over it all. Jahdiel sang the whole song, all verses, including the end refrain 'I prevail, I prevail.' Time stood still. There were no other sounds save for that voice.

When he finished, the Health Visitor's pen also finished its journey to the page. She looked up at him and said, 'You blessed my heart.'

Sleep!

I can do all things through Christ which strengtheneth me.
– Philippians 4:13 KJV

'YOUR CHILD DOESN'T SLEEP THROUGH THE NIGHT?' I looked at the father with pity. A condescending smile was fixed on my face, which I tried desperately to turn into a look of sympathy and camaraderie. Poor thing. They probably did not know what they were doing. He did look a little haggard, with the got-dressed-in-the-dark look and the flitter of a shadow passing across the eyes. We engaged in small talk to get away from the sleep elephant in the room. After a little while, we descended to the old chestnut 'of course we would not change it for the world'.

Maybe I should have shared the benefit of my wisdom. I should have told him about the power of music and how finding the right song might help. Of course, I would haughtily add that we did not need music to help with night sleeping. With my mere few months of fatherly experience, I felt I had graduated to a solid degree, if not to the level of a masters. Perhaps a 2:1 degree if I were being humble, which I was, of course.

That night, Jahdiel's sleep disruption began. I had skipped ahead a couple of chapters in The Book to the chapter on sleep, and was aware of the existence of this creature; sleep disruption. The relevant sections in that chapter had been dutifully underlined for further analysis later on. I did not think, sleep being more or less on track, that those sections would apply to us.

Why had I opened my big mouth? Had I called down the problem by showing off? That very night, Jahdiel woke up at least twice. That was the start of a journey that, even now, so long after the event, brought about flashbacks.

I now know that sleep is what makes the world go round. That much is clear. When sleep is not an issue, you do not realise that you have such a precious gift. Functioning in an automated fog, going through the motions is probably a protective mechanism once that gift has been taken away. The fog of misremembrance. Not remembering doing the baby stuff while half asleep; just seeing the evidence of it in the morning. Even then, that was some comfort. It meant the learning, tough as it might be, was so ingrained

Sleep

it was like walking, like locking the front door. You did not consciously remember locking the door, but on return, both locks were engaged along with the alarm. Still, you kept checking.

It was that world of being careful that the baby was not too tired to sleep. Overtired. Could that happen to the parent, too, of being too tired to sleep? What kind of new level of cruelty was that? The nights started to muddle and blend into one. Did he wake up three times Monday night, or was that Wednesday night? Was I setting a dangerous precedent if I let him fall asleep in my arms? Did that mean I would be forced into that role up until and through his school years?

What was needed was a full recharge. The odd top-up nap now and then got you by, as it must, like going from 16 up to 49% on your mobile or a quick pick me up from 23 to 53% charge, but it plummeted towards empty all too quickly, it seemed, as too many applications had been used.

Every so often, a full recharge was required. Josi was in the same boat, so we tried sleeping in shifts. I once told one of my clients that my representing him was like us being in a boat, rowing in tandem. I was at the front, rowing away, and he was at the back. We both had oars. Sometimes, I would glance back, and he was rowing with me so we could get to our destination all the quicker. Sometimes, when I looked back, he was not rowing at all. Most concerning was when he was not even in the boat helping me to row.

Sometimes, when tiredness was at its most acute, it could feel like we were rowing on our own, although that had never been the case. We just needed more people in the boat to help paddle away.

I scourged our mini library of baby books for the sections on sleep, furiously read the official and creditable sites on the internet over and over for that pearl of wisdom, that magic formula. I delved into unofficial sites, too, but only briefly. There was some scary stuff out there, which is enough to give you nightmares if you could just get a proper amount of sleep.

'He is a boy, so he needs to run around. Take him to the park,' a friend from church mentioned.

That made sense. All children needed fresh air anyway. I prepared lightly—no large baby bag for me. A little side bag contained all the essentials: Jahdiel's water cup topped up with water; baby crackers; oaty bar; small box of raisins; baby bell cheese—that was the snacks covered; wet wipes and tissues, extra clothes. Off we went to the park with Jahdiel on his tricycle, a present from Aunty Dawn. He could pedal it when he wanted to, but I had control with a bar on the back of the bike, which I held or pushed. If he pushed the pedals—when he wanted—it did not turn the wheel unless I wanted it to. Clearly, I was in control.

Sleep

At the park, he had a great time on the slides, swings, pirate ship and climbing frame. Swings were really passive play, which I tried to avoid; he just sat there while Papa did all the work pushing. There were seemingly hundreds of children of various ages dashing off from one apparatus to another. There was a toddler who could barely walk but wanted to climb the stairs to the big slide. I glanced at the father monitoring the feat, but he seemed unconcerned. The bigger boys charged past, seeing the smaller ones as items on an obstacle course and throwing themselves off of equipment onto the fireman poles.

Jahdiel was exhausted after all the fun, which, I think, was the point. He was the right level of tired: too tired to want to remain for one more slide or one more turn on the swing but not too tired that he could not leave the playground under his own steam. What was not in the plan was that he started to fall asleep as we started walking, then tricycling, back home. I clearly did not factor in when sleep was supposed to take place in putting the park plan into action. Still a distance away from home, I had to carry him, and he was not light.

It started to drizzle.

Being up to the task of this aspect of fatherhood, I would not be daunted, and I sang 'Rain, rain, go away' in a jolly undertone with baby on the left shoulder, making sure he was positioned comfortably.

'Are you sleeping, Boog-boog?' I enquired tentatively of him to check if he really was asleep or just pretending.

Giving me a dismissive look with two sleepy eyes, he snuggled further into my shoulder and closed his eyes for what I assumed was the final time. No longer could I see his face as he went full snuggle, and there were sounds of sleep, which I believe told me all I needed to know. My left arm was now totally out of action, fully occupied.

The tricycle was slung over my right shoulder. I properly realised, for the first time, that it was bright blue and white, as though that concept made it lighter; it did not. My right wrist had to be used to hold down the arm of the tricycle, which would have otherwise poked me in the side. I toyed with various permutations as to how else I could position it, including pulling it along, but I rejected them all. For a fraction of a second, I wondered whether I could just leave it in the park and see whether it found its way home. Fine. Right shoulder it is.

There was just enough leverage for the right hand to hold the umbrella I thought to bring. I needed both legs for walking, so they were of no use otherwise. My body parts were no longer my own but props to make this play work.

What I must have looked like! Balanced—just—I started walking in the direction of home. Big sigh. I thought, *I can do this*. Then, there was the unmistakable fragrance of poo. It permeated through his trousers, but the source did not.

Sleep

Yet. I had time then, I thought, but I started walking faster. Frustration built as I reflected that all I wanted when I started this plan was for Jahdiel to be able to sleep peacefully at home. As though he knew that Papa had started to struggle, as if reading my mind or my mood, I heard a sweet angelic voice singing, 'Love is patient, caring, love is kind.' I kissed my teeth – the child was not even sleeping.

But a few minutes later, his head moved down to my shoulder, and his breathing became regular. He had fallen asleep, for sure, this time. I continued my march towards home with renewed purpose. He could not stay in the soiled nappy too long, and now he needed to be put down for his afternoon nap. What time was it? How long until I got home? I had to monitor how long his overall nap was because, well, you had to.

Then, it started to drizzle more. Come on now; really?

I paused mentally, forced myself to enjoy a big sigh and started to embrace the moment. I appreciated, in the moment, at the time, how comic and precious that moment was. It was in that moment I thought that this must have been a part of the joy parents felt, or if they did not, they needed to know about it. I enjoyed the moment and told no one about it at the time. This was fatherhood, I thought, and I smiled as the rain soaked through my fabric loafers (stupid choice that day), through my socks and chilled my feet.

Although the timing needed adjusting, at least the trip to the park had worked. There were many more such visits but without the drama from that experience. Thank you, friend from church, for that advice.

Having done further reading on sleep, I decided it was time to take some more advice from others before we decided what needed to be done. I approached a colleague at work, full of jollity. She would understand. She had children and soon, grandchildren and would acutely know the trauma and drama. She had given me a wonderful book for Jahdiel, *Each Peach Pear Plum* by Janet and Allan Ahlberg, and would clearly be on my side.

I leaned against the door frame to her room. She was a senior member, and there was no one else present, so I could speak freely. I caught her just as she looked up from her papers.

'I had to sleep-train Jahdiel.' I sighed. 'He had to cry a bit, but me waking all night — okay, slight exaggeration — was just not sustainable.' I smiled through my submissions. Surely, that would find favour.

She looked at me dismissively. 'I don't believe in sleep-training babies.'

Oh, shame! I smiled woodenly and sloped off. I ensured that I had no further conversations about sleep around her.

It was nighttime again. I rotated my neck from side to side. I did some lunges and quick breathing calming

Sleep

techniques as I prepared to go upstairs to the baby arena. It was a battle, and I intended to win. We had spoken to a helpful sleep lady recommended by a friend. Sometimes, you just needed third-party assistance. What worked for us was shorter bedtime routines. Speaking to Jahdiel about what was going to happen. Having clear, firm and consistent routines. And frankly, bearing with it. There were, of course, bumps along the road, but it helped us reclaim sleep. And that season, too, passed. The world went round again.

Josi's Reflections

THE DRAMA OF SLEEP IS ONE OF THOSE AREAS WHEN YOU KNOW THAT SOMETIMES, IT IS NOT FUNNY AT THE TIME. Edward, I think, has forgotten a lot of it as a mental protective mechanism. I raised the white flag at some stage in the process while Edward battled on. At the time, Jahdiel was probably wandering into our room at night so much we decided to sleep on the floor of his bedroom for a few nights. That was where the situation took us, which was some time on the journey towards sleep. Visiting my mother one day, it was the Grace of God that led me back home, packaged as it was with Edward, with Jahdiel in his arms, saying as I left, 'Love you. Make sure you come back.'

The advice from The Book, the internet and family and friends were varied, and it felt like we tried them all.

'Swaddling,' said one source. 'So he feels comfort all around him like being in the womb.'

'Use a mobile over his cot,' proclaimed one friend. 'The movement and sound will lull him to sleep.'

'A good feed before bed is what helps.' The speaker tried to load their words with gravitas.

'He needs a sleep sheep, of course,' said another, as though nothing could be simpler.

'Give him a bath before bedtime and a nice massage, and he will go right off to bed and sleep until morning,' one aunty with children and grandchildren suggested.

'The smell of lavender, that is what works,' declared another with such confidence.

'Do not pick him up as you are enabling him,' cautioned a cousin.

Cross, cross, cross and cross off the list.

Was it his way of rebelling or a form of protest? Was he saying, 'I want you around me now and all the time?' How could it be otherwise when there was an occasion when his intense crying made him throw up? That meant we had to go into his room, turn on the lights, take him out of his cot, change him and change the bed sheets, so bedtime was delayed. The cream carpet had evidence of the last two meals, I think, as the huge pack of cleaning wipes we

Sleep

bought came into its own. Among the busyness of cleaning the floor, the wall, the bed and thinking of the look the washing machine would give me yet again for its overuse, I glanced at Jahdiel; the child was grinning!

Sometimes, the guidance from different sources just conflicted. In what position should a baby be put to sleep? The guidance now seemed to have changed from that given years ago. And it was different from suggestions from family members in our Caribbean countries. My family was getting frustrated by our refusal to put into action what they recommended when we complained about sleep difficulties. 'But this is the United Kingdom,' we would say, 'and the recommendation is for a baby to sleep in a certain position.'

That same toddler sleeping bag with holes for his legs, which was a part of the ecstatic joy of having his own toddler bed, just meant he was snuggly and warm as he made his way to our bedroom throughout the night. So, yes—there was no crying, but there was something about being woken up in the middle of the night by a silhouette saying, 'Papa' that could not but send chills down our backs. Edward would jump out of bed.

Not to be defeated, Edward slept on the floor of Jahdiel's bedroom, then, in time, transitioned to sleep in the chair in the room. Then Edward progressed—as that was what we hoped it was—to sleeping outside his door. He told me tales of waiting in Jahdiel's darkened room for the sound of regular breathing, meaning he had finally—finally—fallen asleep, of crawling on hands and knees quietly—quietly—as he exited the room, making sure the hinges on the door were well oiled so he would not be betrayed by a squeak as the door was opened, millimetre by precious millimetre until he could make his escape. He stepped lightly back to our room so the floorboards would not squeak even though they were covered by carpet. We did not know how long the whole process had taken, by the time we spoke to the sleep lady.

It was never-ending because it overlapped with the colic and the skin challenges. It sat at the same time as the lactose-free milk to see if there was intolerance. With checking stool samples. All of that came and went but sleep continued. Other parents saying their child slept through the night did not help, but if that was your path, be thankful for the gift that it was!

Edward has forgotten these things. I think he buried them deep as they were layers of, I do not know what exactly, in that season. They have been blocked out. He forgot that he questioned how he was now sleeping on the floor when he paid the bills for the home. The dark circles under his eyes told their own story.

Sometimes, you forgot that this, too, shall pass. Sometimes, you needed outside assistance, but culturally, that was not what we did. It was during the COVID lockdowns, so there were virtual meetings and exchanging of messages and feedback afterwards with the sleep consultant. She was, after all, like the nurses at hospital who helped with feeding, the Health Visitor who gave guidance on care, the general practitioner who gave the needed injections. They were all a part of our army of support, different to family and friends but invaluable in their own way, so we felt no guilt making her part of our army.

I would only later—much later—find out that various family and friends had challenges around sleep with their own children when they were babies and toddlers. Sometimes, you needed to know that others—directly from those others—had been through it and survived, that they, too, had been in the trenches. Sometimes, what you needed was not advice and remedies but to know that others had been in the wilderness, too. Maybe we would not have been able to listen. What I do know is we did not have the presence of mind to ask, 'What was it like for you, Cousin, Aunty, Uncle?' at the time.

And that, too, did pass. Some things you perhaps just had to go through. One of the solutions for these things was patience. But we can be clear: it was not like those moments I wanted to bottle and revisit. Yes, aspects were now chuckle-funny in hindsight in the same way you let out a big breath you did not know you were holding.

I take a big breath, and I can smile. Now.

Child Care

Fathers, provoke not your children to anger, lest they be discouraged.
– Colossians 3:21 KJV

YOU DO NOT KNOW YOU HAVE CLAWS UNTIL YOU FEEL YOUR CHILD HAS BEEN WRONGED. Your anger is pure because it is for your little one and not for yourself. Your little one is not able to defend himself, not able to fight for himself, and you do not want the little one to fight for himself because you want to preserve his innocence as long as possible. You do not want him to be aware of the source of your ire. The anger is so intense that you go beyond it and become calm. That is when you have an insight into the behaviours of the animal kingdom, how they fight to protect their young.

There is much I would have probably let pass if it were directed at me, little cuts that might, in time, come together to cause a big bleed. They were avoided because of the knowledge of how to apply plasters and bandages every so often to stem the flow. But not when it came to our child. And so, we wanted to ensure that those who surrounded him, those who would be his carers, cared enough for him to take on some of that concern on his behalf. That they, too, would have claws and anger on his behalf when needed. You assume that family and friends, properly so called, would care for him as if he were their own, that they would fight for him.

How precious it was to have clawed-up family and friends where you lived to allow the parents a much-needed rest. That army of grandparents who got stuck in and took care of your little ones as and when, need to be celebrated. I saw them doing the nursery and school drop-offs, collecting the little ones from nursery because Mummy and Daddy were at work or attending to something equally important, including paying bills. Or just having some time off; also important. That team of aunts and uncles embracing the sharp learning curve of nappy changes, eating routines and bedtime stories to allow Mama and Papa time to just breathe. Let us stop, pause and applaud that army.

That army meant you could embrace your absence when not with your little one as he was safe. Embrace the absence

Child Care

that really did make the heart grow fonder. Not the absence of five minutes while Mama or Papa had a cup of tea with the hope that the toddler would entertain himself. No. This was an absence of a few hours or—the holy grail—an overnight (dare we say two?) away from Mama and Papa. That time fully allowed and entitled me to rush to scoop up my little one afterwards, as that one overnight felt like a whole week of not having seen him. I hugged him tightly and spun him around as if I had not seen him for days or weeks. 'I've missed you,' I would say. Whether or not he replied, 'Missed you, Papa,' or even more exquisite, if he initiated the miss you dialogue, my cup would runneth over.

'I'll take care of him any time' was, therefore, the most beautiful proclamation family or friends could give. And we heard it often from those family or FamilyFriends properly so called. Not Aunty Annie or Uncle Ugbert or Cousin Connie (not their real names), who hid a multitude of negativity behind the facade of a smile, who spoke with forked tongues and brought the knife as well. No, I speak of those who looked to his best interests. Who supported us. Whose celebration of our successes were genuine and as if those successes were their own, and indeed, they were. Those with the claws.

FamilyFriends are friends who are like family, who have crossed the biological rubicon into the inner sphere. They can come to your house, sit on your sofa, use your shower and have access to the good towels.

All of that was great. Thank you, FamilyFriends. But you know our child is particular. We were clearly the first parents in history who properly entrusted their child to family or FamilyFriends, so we had to be careful when stepping into that previously unchartered territory.

One of the first times we said yes to the offer of care was when Aunty Dawn was there for the evening. We had a birthday dinner to attend; an important birthday: the fortieth.

The meetings with Aunty Dawn about the event were a series of conversations, both in person and by telephone. There may or may not have been an agenda for the meetings. There may or may not have been minutes taken at the meeting. I will confirm there were dry runs of what would happen on the night itself. Jahdiel was to be cared for at home, so there were not too many unknowns to the routine. It was explained to him that Aunty Dawn would be with him that night, and that would be fun. He agreed as he was a big fan of Aunty Dawn, anyway. That was why she was strategically selected.

Tolerant as always, Aunty Dawn patiently submitted to the lengthy preparations for the night itself. She was kind enough not to point out that the preparations were wholly disproportionate to the purpose. She smiled graciously

Child Care

as we went through the very many steps involved in the bedtime routine again. It was an evening dinner we were going to, after all. It would go on past his bedtime, so Aunty Dawn was informed of the time for bedtime, which pyjamas he wore and the order in which each item of clothing had to be put on, how to put on his nappy properly and the optimum amount of Bepanthan cream to avoid nappy rash and irritation. She was warned about his cunning tricks to avoid sleeping in favour of prolonging play.

The instructions, I suspected, would fill a small manual: The Book II.

It was only after she had been fully briefed that we discovered Aunty Dawn was fully aware of many aspects of Jahdiel's care. On one of the days after instruction but before the day of the event, Aunty Dawn was visiting us as she often did. I was busy somewhere in the house doing something very important, no doubt. Best not to ask what; let's just agree that it was important.

Josi told me this story shortly afterwards. She, Aunty Dawn and Jahdiel were in the kitchen. Jahdiel had the look on his face that meant a non-surprise was shortly expected in his nappy. Mama was juggling something in the kitchen, and changing Jahdiel just could not be made a part of that juggling. She looked pleadingly at Aunty Dawn. I can only imagine the unspoken dialogue that took place between the two of them.

I imagined Mama projecting to Aunty Dawn: 'I know you have never changed a nappy before, but this is an emergency. Please.' I imagined the flicker in Aunty Dawn's eyes as she assessed the depth of the smell, the expansion of the nappy. I like to think what won out was that she was one of many who wanted a nephew, and so felt obliged to step up and help! I suspected she sighed or humphed or a combination of the two before accepting the inevitable. The whole unspoken conversation likely lasted only seconds.

Upstairs she went with Jahdiel. After a couple of minutes of silence, a lull in the kitchen juggle allowed Mama to go upstairs to see whether she could assist. I do not know, and there was no confirmation, so I cannot say that Mama sprinted upstairs to see what was happening. She looked into Jahdiel's bedroom from the doorway. She caught her breath and paused before entering. It was that pause that betrayed Aunty Dawn because Mama observed a truly startling scene.

I feel as if I've seen the event fully through Mama's eyes, as she has told me of the events many times. The room was bathed with light. It was early afternoon, and it was a relatively clear day. No brilliant sunshine, but enough to fill the room with illumination without artificial light. Jahdiel's cot stood on one side of the room. The baby camera was in another corner, surveying the space, angled as best as we could to capture the main part of the room: the cot, the

Child Care

wardrobe, some of the floor and the drawer on which the changing mat sat. In her flight through the kitchen and up the traitorous stairs to Jahdiel's room, Mama forgot that she could have used the baby cam to observe the proceedings. Or maybe the baby cam was too much like being a voyeur. Or maybe the need to see events in the flesh was at the forefront of her mind.

The surprise at the end of her adrenaline-filled pursuit, when her mind was either on other things or not expecting what had actually taken place, was acute. Mama surveyed the scene, taking in everything at once, her mind analysing it all in a fraction of a second, wanting to rush in to interrupt that truly startling scene, forcing herself not to interrupt although desperately, urgently, wanting to.

Aunty Dawn's back was to Mama, but the angle of the door and the proximity of the changing table cruelly betrayed Aunty Dawn, making the scene clear to Mama. And to me through Mama's eyes.

She—we—observed a truly startling scene: Aunty Dawn was changing Jahdiel's nappy as though she had done it hundreds of times before, as Jahdiel smiled at her conspiratorially. He did not realise Mama was at the door. They were speaking to each other in the Aunty Dawn-Jahdiel language, for which there was no dictionary. It was as if they were in a world of their own, and there was a distinct impression that it was not the first time it had happened.

Sometimes It's Funny

It seemed to last for hours, those few minutes. When they eventually realised that eyes other than the baby cam had observed the proceedings, the look of humour on Aunty Dawn's face seemed mirrored on Jahdiel's; their secret had been discovered.

Even after that incident, the briefing continued for the evening Aunty Dawn was going to babysit, though with a different tone as we realised Aunty Dawn had more knowledge than we realised. There were insights from that truly startling scene, which Aunty Dawn laughed off, finding the situation funny. We did not find it funny. We thought of the countless times a baby changing was required when we rushed to do the changing as Aunty Dawn looked on. I cannot kiss my teeth long or hard enough.

On the evening of the babysitting for the fortieth birthday dinner, of course, Jahdiel knew something was different. Mama and Papa were dressed up. Aunty Dawn was still at our home and did not look as if she were going anywhere. It all confirmed that what Mama and Papa had said about Aunty Dawn staying with him that evening was true. He happily said goodbye to us and played with Aunty Dawn.

Aunty Dawn told us that after we left, things initially went well. Slowly, he realised that we were not there, and the tears started. Aunty Dawn soldiered on; the tears were his and not hers. She did the bedtime routine but then went off-piste by falling asleep in his room. That event was,

Child Care

at least, new to her. There were no secret evenings when she cared for Jahdiel; there was no secret practice run.

And I cheated. I saw it all on the baby camera. While everyone else was singing 'Happy Birthday to You' in the restaurant, I was looking into the monitor on the app on my mobile, singing words I did not believe were in any verse of any happy birthday song, trying to multitask... badly. I used any slight pretext in conversations at the dinner table to segue into tales of Jahdiel, which clearly required me to look at the monitor to emphasise my point. By the time we got to dessert—ice cream and chocolate cake—I had settled down somewhat. Do not ask what the main course was since I was multitasking at the time. I barely remembered eating it.

Since then, of course, other FamilyFriends have baby- and toddler-sat for Jahdiel.

Aunty Mich did so on one memorable occasion during the day so Josi and I could have a date day. By that time, we realised that the briefings to FamilyFriends could be conversations that did not require an agenda. No one needed to take notes or text to confirm understanding!

Again, so there would be as much familiarity as possible, Aunty Mich and her daughter came to our house to care for Jahdiel, who once more had the home advantage. We said goodbye to him, and then we were off. He hardly seemed to notice and was not concerned. As the front door closed,

I noticed that he rushed off to continue playing Simon Says with Aunty Mich and her daughter. Okay, we did not want him to be traumatised by our leaving, but we wanted him to at least pretend he was going to miss us!

We would build to other occasions where we'd leave Jahdiel in the care of FamilyFriends. In time. We dipped into the army now and then.

***

It was a whole other creature when the childcare came in the form of a nursery. The assumption was that there was a minimum of expertise required and therefore, a minimum reassurance when your child was at nursery. There were certain standards, were there not? Certificates meeting Ofsted ratings. To work in a nursery, you'd think the staff must love children to have chosen to be surrounded by a number of precious, fragile beings for the whole day, every day, while maintaining whatever pep and positivity was required for the long haul. They had to have chosen to change nappies containing a whole spectrum of smells and consistencies, to wipe little Johnny's nose, to make sure little Janie did not swallow item X or throw item Y. It was exhausting just thinking of all the macro and micro considerations for nursery practitioners.

Looking for the right nursery felt like choosing the right university: doing the research, creating graphs and charts

Child Care

with the pros and cons of each establishment, getting soundings from people and parents in the area, going into a world we did not know existed. I had lived in the area of our home for many years and had no idea about the world of choosing a nursery. I'd had no prior reason to swim in those currents.

We went round visiting the various establishments, putting in our applications, though it was clear we might not get into the one we wanted anyway. We feared seeing a nursery that would have kept the children like animals, where there would be cots stacked up like crates, piled one on top of the other in the room for naptime. We feared having members of staff looking out at the parents coming to view the nursery with the vacant expression of someone who has realised that working in a nursery was not what they were led to believe, and now, they were tied into a mind-destroying routine or lack of routine.

We did not want such an environment to be inflicted on Jahdiel. Artificial though it might be, I wanted him surrounded by raindrops and roses, staff who smiled from the moment Jahdiel entered the nursery until their last wave goodbye at him, an environment saturated with life, learning and laughter that nurtured his curiosity and built his confidence. These were child experts, so he must come home steeped in their expertise after being exposed to nature and knowledge, friends and frolics. All of that and more should come from those oh-so-expensive nurseries. And he might as well pick up words from another language while he was there.

We found a nursery with a great outdoor space. His key worker was friendly. The atmosphere was even friendlier, fresh food cooked every day for the children, we were told. There would be support in feeding and support in potty training if that was the parents' wish. Jahdiel would be settled into the nursery at his own pace; the choir sang, the orchestra played and all was well.

We did not know that in two years' time, we would be scrambling to get out faster than we had scrambled to get in. We did not know that we would be part of a cadre of parents united in the need to just... get... out. Nor did we know that the much-loved outdoor space, with its weeping willow, would not cry in laughter with us, but for us. Our wiser, two years older selves looked back at us with knowing smiles.

Only one child looked to be of Caribbean or African descent at the nursery. That child was no longer there on the second day after Jahdiel started, but I barely registered those facts. I rationalised them, like the NCT class, as a consequence of the location of the nursery. I did not learn of the 2001 United States study that asserted that children as young as three had been observed to 'employ racial and ethnic concepts as important integrative and symbolically

Child Care

creative tools in the daily construction of their social lives'[3] until much later. Why would I have thought the issue of racial concepts relevant to nursery? Our experiences at the nursery included a toddler asking Josi whether she was the mummy of a younger toddler. This was said with an innocence that melted our hearts. Neither toddler had the same skin tone as Josi, nor did they otherwise look like her. We were justified in thinking, were we not, that conscious racialisation was many years in the future.

Therefore, at the time of Jahdiel's starting the nursery, the nursery seemed ideal without this future knowledge.

With all our research, visits, conversations and everything else, we forgot to convince Jahdiel that it was ideal. Again, we were making assumptions for him. He did not take separating from us well initially. Okay, that was a huge understatement. He cried a lot and distressed his allocated staff member. Her reaction, of course, did not help. It was not good. That look of absolute betrayal on his face as we attempted to moonwalk out of the room was not easy.

We started to rethink the idea of both parents working, but he settled. Of course, he did. And we settled. Of course, we did; we had to. The way in for Jahdiel, like many things, was music. We sang on the way to the nursery and asked the staff to keep singing that and other songs as he was

---

3   Van Ausdale, D., & Feagin, J. R. (2001) *The first R: How children learn race and racism.* Rowman and Littlefield.

handed over. That seemed to work. It was only then that we could drop him off and leave hand in hand on our child-is-at-nursery date, on the walk home from the nursery. Then we transitioned away from needing to call the nursery 5, 10 minutes after leaving to check whether he'd settled.

A few short months after the start of Jahdiel's journey in nursery, lockdowns began in the United Kingdom. The problem that was elsewhere, someone else's problem, became our own as a nation. We all saw that bear coming but in our arrogance, thought it wouldn't bite us. Our noses were too high to see the reality on the ground.

A few years before, I had joked with Aunty Dawn about our noses being too high to see the reality on the ground. I told her about the time I went to Pret a Manger for a sandwich and coffee. It was its usual busy, catering, as it did, to workers in central London where I was based for work. I paid with cash — such a thing still existed — and I did not notice that a five-pound note had fallen from my wallet onto the ground in front of the counter.

I walked back to work less than five minutes away, blissfully unaware that I was five pounds lighter, only feeling the lack of that weight when I got into our building after climbing to the second floor and settling down to eat at my desk. Five pounds being more than I could spare, I rushed back with a prayer in my head but minuscule hope in my heart, retracing my steps.

Child Care

Sniffing canine-like, my eyes were peeled to the ground as I retraced my steps, not knowing for sure when that traitorous note had made its escape. I walked sprightly into Pret—I could not be seen running, as that was not the done thing—arriving after what felt like an hour of being away; it was, at most, 10 minutes.

There it lay, in front of the very counter at which I had paid for the sandwich and coffee, both snacks having been unceremoniously left to get cold on my desk. There, it lay undisturbed, carefree, waiting for me. No one in the still-busy establishment looked at it. I bent down, retrieved it and returned it home.

'Their noses were too high in the air to look down,' I later joked with Aunty Dawn. Was it too small a note for someone to take? Was the tunnel vision of getting in, buying and getting out too intense to allow for other unexpected stimuli? I would like to think it was being protected for me and, therefore, unseen by all except me. What it did, was make me take stock every so often as to the height of my nose.

Disbelieving, or whatever, the view taken of COVID's progress and the hows and whys, come, it did. My nose, like many it seemed, had remained too high.

But for that period of COVID, I would not have gathered the memories detailed below. Those stories would have been for others to tell. I would have been, on the balance of probability, sent somewhere around greater London, or indeed, England, for work. The world of baby breakfasts and bath routines would not have been mine. Looking back now, we were grateful for the forced family time that enabled us to see those micro Jahdiel steps. The stock of family memories that cannot be taken away. Nurturing and teaching and playing with Jahdiel and each other because we had to, became nurturing and teaching and playing because we wanted to.

As time passed, Jahdiel was able to return to nursery, being a key worker's child. Both of us worked and cared for him first before he could return, and when he did, it brought challenges of time and patience. We'd made it work because we had to. We'd reframed the narrative because we had to, as a sign that we needed to spend time together as a family. That we needed to park what was not and embrace what was. It was in this period that we saw how much of a sponge Jahdiel was for learning, and we poured into that sponge. Letters, numbers, everything: we poured.

But for that period of forced family time, I would not have known for myself that as Jahdiel progressed from the baby room to the toddler room to the main room, he made one, then two, firm friends. His *best friends*, he said. He started to really enjoy nursery and the exposure it gave him. It was from there that one of my most precious nursery moments came.

Child Care

When doing the pick-ups from nursery during lockdown, I had to wait at the main door. He was brought to the door with his going home bag and any dirty clothes. The door opened. He saw me and a huge smile took over his face.

'Papa!' he shouted and ran into my arms. There were only the two of us in the world at that point. I loved nursery pick-up just for those moments, the exquisite happiness on his face day to day. Those moments, I bottled and shelved to be taken out whenever I needed to swim in bliss.

I learnt the names of the other babies, then the toddlers, in the nursery. The staff member Jahdiel used to throw up on was in the baby room. It was good he'd transitioned out of that stage before he moved out of the baby room, as there was starting to be a degree of strain in her eyes whenever Jahdiel arrived at the nursery. It was beginning to develop into a degree of panic. The relief in those same eyes was getting a little too evident on pick-up. The day she had on the same clothes in the afternoon as in the morning, she had an extra spring in her step. Or had I imagined that?

In the toddler room, Jahdiel had more freedom. He had some great key workers who spoke to us about building his confidence, about how he was developing well. There were useful meetings with the managers if we had any concerns so we could work collaboratively. He remained the only child in the nursery who looked like him, which, for us, added another layer of challenge, although we initially did not think it would be so. One or two others joined but then disappeared before we had the chance to speak to their parents.

It slowly became possible to put faces to the names Jahdiel mentioned at home to establish whether they were toddlers or staff members. That became easier as he went from the toddler room to the main room, the room for the oldest children at the nursery.

In the main room, the toddlers got increasingly used to me.

'What's your name?' one particularly precocious child asked. Another asked the same on another occasion. Whether inside the nursery or during drop off or pick up, they seemed to like that particular question.

My answer was always the same: 'Jahdiel's papa.' I did not pander to that first-name nonsense. *I am not your age little one*, I thought. We are not school friends. Kindly of me, I did not go so far as to say 'Mr Flood'. Growing up in Saint Lucia, any adult's first name was always said with a prefix, either 'Ms' or 'Mr', or they had some kind of appellation like 'teacher'. I would never have thought to call any adult by their first name, without prefix or appellation. It was just... not... done.

'Jahdiel's Papa, Jahdiel's Papa—where is Jahdiel going?' asked the precocious child, the same one who'd asked me

Child Care

my name before. I'd had the temerity to collect Jahdiel early to go to a dentist appointment.

Too shocked at the question, I told her the truth: 'He's going to the dentist.'

She looked at me, clearly judging whether my answer was a proper reason to remove Jahdiel from the important event that was play. She gave me permission to continue walking Jahdiel to the car. Her expression, which followed me with her eyes, head unmoving, made it equally clear that the conversation was not over. There would be further exploration on other issues in due course.

As lockdown eased, parents were allowed to go into the rooms to collect their children. That brought with it a whole new world. I could see properly, rather than imagine, the various things Jahdiel was chatty about when he got home. It made me realise that we were not fostering enough of his independence at home. In the nursery, he could take off his own jacket, hat and scarf and put them on his dedicated peg. The infamous 'decking' was made a reality for me. It was the wooden deck at the back of the nursery, which Jadhiel would often mention, where the children could play. The toys of which much had been made were introduced to me in the flesh, or rather, in the plastic.

Going inside the main room to collect Jahdiel, I was often surrounded by his toddler friends. They had all moved on from the days of surprise over my knowing and greeting them with their names. One was a few months younger than him. I was tempted to clean the snot pouring from her nose as none of the practitioners seemed to have noticed. Thinking better of it, I proclaimed loudly that her nose was running and suggested one of the staff members might wish to consider dealing with it. There were germs afoot, after all.

Another was a second precocious little girl approaching four years old. Let us call her Sally. Sally was best friends with the precocious little girl who'd asked my name and given me a pass to collect Jahdiel early. That background knowledge should have warned me. One of the practitioners — when did they stop simply being called 'helpers' or 'teachers'? — told me our son had done a little painting. I looked for it and found a painting in his cubby hole. Surrounded by toddlers, including my son and Sally, I thought I'd better be and sound child-appropriate and friendly. They were all, I am sure, listening.

'Oh, is this your painting, son?' I asked, my voice dripping with positivity and good cheer. The smile on my face could not have been any more welcoming or sunny.

Sally looked at me without a trace of humour on her face. I smiled at her, expecting cuteness.

'Does it have his name on it?' Sally asked in a deadpan voice. It was not quite a question and said with a voice that

Child Care

must have taken at least 35 years to master, more a statement of indisputable fact.

'Yes,' I said cheerfully, as it did have his name of it.

'Then it's his,' she responded in that same 35-year marinated voice. She wandered off finished with me, and my smile withered.

Shame. I calmly and quietly collected my child and left the building. There was nothing quite so humbling as being put in your place by an almost-four-year-old.

Sure, there were teething problems — with the nursery, not Jahdiel. There were cracks. There was a special category and level of anxiety when, at one minute past two o'clock on a Tuesday afternoon at work, there was a call from the nursery on my mobile. A conversation needed to take place, ensuring that such calls should really only be for genuine emergencies. Otherwise, it could wait until the end of the day, could it not? I could not know that was the beginning of more cracks to come, so innocent it seemed at the time.

***

I often compared childcare in London with childcare in Saint Lucia. Childcare when I was young in Saint Lucia was more than nursery, more than FamilyFriends. Saint Lucia itself, its very air, helped raise us, Aunty Dawn and me. That sweet air outsiders might think we took for granted, the reality being that we took full advantage of it. Oh, gosh, we enjoyed it! The sun smiled down on us; the rain nourished us as it did the soil.

My sister and I grew up in the country in Saint Lucia, in Desruisseaux. The rivers and streams were our playgrounds. Making pots out of clay that we baked in our grandmother's oven without telling her. The lush green vegetation. Forests that seemed endless. Adventures exploring the neighbours' land. Picking passion fruit, mangoes, guavas, and tamarind from the fruit trees and eating them as we ran as we did not know on whose land we'd trespassed.

It was a serious sun in the bright sunshine, the air so clear you could see for miles all the way to the beach from inland. From the south of the island, you could see the island of Saint Vincent in the distance. From the north, the island of Martinique. A flash of lightning and its thunder companion created excitement for my sister and me like no other. We knew the rain wanted to be as powerful as the sun was strong. The anticipation was exquisite, knowing the delight that was to come.

Rain. Heavy rain. What could be sweeter than the sound of rain falling at night on a galvanise roof while lying in bed? The music of the water aggressively striking that roof was a symphony to beat no other. We closed our eyes and breathed deeply as we basked in the experience.

In the day, if there was ordinary rain without lightning in evidence, Mum would let us put on our swimming

Child Care

costumes, go outside and bathe in the rain. We would run and dance in the rain. Then freeze in place, closing our eyes. Tilting our head back to feel that wonderful warm shower fully on our eyelids, cheeks and forehead. I was transported back. We missed it so much, Aunty Dawn and I, that in our young adulthood in London, we bought CDs of thunderstorms and rainforests, trying to recapture those magical moments.

We did not have that rain in London — how would we let Jahdiel know how to dance in the rain without the rain? Jahdiel would not have the opportunity to be cared for by the land as I was — should I take him back home for a period of time to have that kind of childcare?

Even schooling in Saint Lucia was so different to Jahdiel's experiences in London. My grandmother, Euriza James, ran a preschool near where we lived. We called her Mama. She would go on to be awarded an MBE for her contribution to the community, including that preschool, but in those pre-MBE years, that school building was just another playground during the holidays. It sat smugly under a vast mango tree, as if knowing of the award that would come. Its wooden walls, only 15 feet away from Mama's house, had protected an army of school children since Mama was about 18 years old when she'd started the school. It continued until she decided to do less in her eighties.

Did she really do less, then? She would still take morning prayers. The children would still chant, 'C-A-T... cat. B-A-T... bat,' under her stern direction. I think it was only when she died, at 93 and a half years old, that she finally, definitively, retired. At the end, like at the start, age was also measured in months and weeks.

I was among that army of children. That preschool, that foundation of learning, attracted young children from all over the community and beyond. Parents sent their children, although technically a little too young to start at preschool. It heaved at full capacity in those days. Children spilt out of the doors at break time, lunchtime, home time, scattering to all parts of the yard. Mama's chicken coop, just next to it, was a place of excitement and danger. That was the poultry which would cock-a-doodle-doo my sister and me awake in the mornings when we slept some nights with Mama. The roosters perched in the tamarind tree next to the coop, and only the bravest children dared climb to pick tamarinds under their accusing gaze. It was eerie as only their heads moved over their frozen bodies to watch the climber.

We learned the rudiments of all things school in that preschool, more than just how to count and recite and sing spelling at the tops of our voices. With its concrete floor and galvanised roof, with its outside toilet and benches without backs so children wobbled and almost fell off if they fell asleep in class. Mama would have ice blocks and

Child Care

icicles for sale, but often, she just gave them to the children without the parents needing to pay.

We graduated all too soon to go on to 'big school', Desruisseaux Combined School, the primary school up the road. I did not know—how could I?—that a few years later, when we went back to England, educationally, I would be over a year further ahead of my classmates in London.

With nursery and schooling in London, it sometimes seemed that we had to pay privately for the kind of education I automatically got as a right in Saint Lucia. Such schooling in Saint Lucia also seemed of a higher quality.

Was there a higher value on education back home than our experience of education here in London? Did we expect too much of nursery, catering, as it did, to children before they turned five years old? Was learning in Saint Lucia just a moment in time, out of time, and was it unfair to compare? But for the shock that my 10-year-old self felt at the simple things my London classmates did not know, I would have thought I had over-romanticised my time in the Helen of the West.

Learning through play was a bedrock of the early years' narrative in the United Kingdom. Coming, as I did, from a structured education system in Saint Lucia, where we had learning through structured education from preschool, I viewed such a bedrock with a hefty degree of scepticism. Children are sponges—why not feed them, was my feeling, with proper education. He could play at home, after all. Was I alone? Did parents who grew up in the Caribbean, as I had, prefer a more structured approach to learning for their children?

We desperately searched for another nursery for Jahdiel. The cracks that ill thought-through telephone call represented became crevices when he moved to the main room. The rapid turnover of staff, a national problem, was becoming more acute because of inadequate handovers from one staff member to another. The new staff did not know Jahdiel. We had meetings with management. I spoke in a casual way of my concerns with the staff. We became increasingly aware that other parents were likewise growing dissatisfied. Children had been leaving the nursery before they needed to, and we now understood why, and we wanted to do the same. It was great in the baby room and in the toddler room, but it was time to move on.

'What did you do today at nursery?' we asked Jahdiel.

'Running around,' became the consistent reply. Young Edward would never have said that of Mama's preschool in Saint Lucia. How much running around could they do in that open space? He'd learned so much, being with us at home during lockdown, but he was stagnating at nursery. We could not countenance him remaining there until the academic year he turned five.

He had to get out.

Child Care

Josi's Reflections

A GENERAL PRACTITIONER ONCE SAID TO ME THAT CARING FOR A CHILD AND WORKING IS—NOT IS LIKE, BUT IS—HAVING TWO FULL-TIME JOBS. I had not looked at it like that before. He explained that your job finished at a certain time. Caring for your child psychologically, if not physically, started a minute after your job ended and continued until the next time your job started again. Then there was the overlap. Your job may or may not feature in your mind at times when you are caring for your child, being present with your child, trying to fully nurture your child, but it is very likely your child featured in your mind throughout the time you were at work. Was that working two full-time jobs with overtime for each?

The lesson continued: caring for your child full time, when you have stopped or paused from your formal work, was a full-time job. It could be more intense than going out to work. You might not have the luxury of a tea break when you want it. Bathroom breaks were not when your body demanded but when a little person allowed. Speaking to your adult employer or yourself, if you worked for yourself, about the need for a little break to recharge and replenish, which you were kindly allowed, was a contracted dream. Your little employer took no nonsense about your needing downtime when you needed it. Your little employer allowed you that courtesy if and when he deemed you were not required for a moment or, frankly, never.

I echoed my thanks to the FamilyFriends who knew the spirit, if not the articulation, of those sentiments from the general practitioner. Those who reached out to say, 'I will lend a hand,' or even better, those who said, 'Of course, I can care for him,' when we initiated the come-on-you-must dialogue! You were invaluable, and long may that continue!

Grandma dipped her toe into that river of childcare and realised the Jahdiel energy currents ran quite fast.

'Jahdi, Jahdi!' she called out to him and followed him around as he toddled through her garden. After that excitement was done, he wanted to go upstairs. And tap on the keyboard. And then downstairs. Then, back in the garden. And then... and then. I saw the pep of the initial 'Jahdi, Jahdi' from oh, so long ago (15 minutes) start to wane.

Nennenn (godmother in Kweyol) took him out sometimes. Her experience as a teacher meant she had researched caring for toddlers in advance, by implication.

As Jahdiel transitioned into nursery, we realised that it was, more or less, what was referred to on the nursery's website as expensive childcare. And doubly so. As I nursed Jahdiel from yet another ailment, which meant he could not be at nursery (the rules were strict about that), I reflected on the irony that he most likely picked up the germs from the

Child Care

very same nursery. Who called nurseries havens of disease or disease cesspools? I'd better not say. It increasingly felt that we were paying the nursery for the privilege of keeping Jahdiel home, as another loose stool signalled yet another 48 hours for him to be kept at home.

For a fever, I gave him Calpol, some baby medication. As the liquid drained drop by drop into his mouth, my hope of him going to nursery in the morning likewise drained away, drop by drop. Another rule: he could not go to nursery if he had Calpol the night before.

Edward started to tally up the number of days he was at home compared to the days in the nursery. That was not a helpful exercise, so I turned my face away from the calendar and calculator.

I felt sure the term 'childcare' did not exist when I was growing up in Montserrat. The community, the village, got involved. If a parent wanted to go to the shops, they just left their child or children with a family member or a neighbour. There was a knowing of the people around you, the spirit of us all being in this together.

Edward spoke of *koudmen* in Saint Lucia, everyone chipping in to help with a group project, like restoring a neighbour's house. There would be no call for payment, maybe just refreshments and food for all involved. Although we did not have that Kweyol word in Montserrat, the sentiment was clearly there. It had been translated, in the limited way it could, to all of us here in London, England. *Koudmen* faced challenges here in an alien environment, battling forces of suspicion, otherness and stiff upper lips that prepared you for this world but might not have a smile of welcome.

And so, as for the projects, the same goes for the children. Nanny—or Grandma or Uncle or Aunty—in Montserrat looked after the children when the parents went to work. When a neighbour collected their own child from school, so would they collect yours if your child was still at school and the neighbour was passing by your house anyway. It was not often spoken about, just known and done. Or, if spoken about, simply said in passing.

'Josi is finishing school at 3 p.m. While you're going by the school on the way to the shop, pick her up for me, yes?' This was said by my grandmother, who barely looked at the neighbour or paused from sweeping the yard. Similarly, the listening neighbour took the suggestion in a light way, the unnecessary request barely acknowledged as she continued walking past my grandmother. She was planning to collect Josi anyway, as my grandmother was obviously busy.

On another occasion, another neighbour, whose child was in the same school, might say to the teacher at the end of the school day, 'Miss, I'll take her. She can stay with me until her grandmother comes home.'

Child Care

Edward spoke of his grandmother, who had the preschool in Saint Lucia. Many times, the children just stayed on with his grandmother after school because the parents had yet to collect their children. They were delayed due to traffic, work or the many little time battles that resulted in lateness. She just gave them dinner if it was getting too late.

My older cousins took me to school; my grandmother did not even have to think about that being done. They braided my hair because it needed doing, not because they had specifically been asked. They did not have to be asked. The idea that those cousins, those relatives, those neighbours might seek payment was anathema. The very idea that Edward's grandmother in Saint Lucia would ask for a further fee for after-school care because she'd provided dinner was laughable.

Discipline was a shared responsibility. In Montserrat, as young children, we refrained from misbehaving, even when our parents and carers were not around. We knew the community would deal with us if we stepped out of line. They had the licence to do so. And then they would let our parents—who would also deal with us—know. It was then I properly valued those precious things from back home that we took for granted.

Childcare? Ha! As children, everyone cared for us.

Every Hair on Your Head

Even the very hairs on your head are all numbered.
– Luke 12:7 KJV

'I DON'T LIKE IT,' HE SCREAMED. Again. 'I don't like washing my hair.' There were no tears in his eyes as he sat in the bath. His hair complaint was the perfect moment to remind him that he would soon have a nice haircut. That it would look lovely, just like the boy in church with the short hair.

'But when I cut my hair, I'll have no hair.' It was his usual complaint.

'You will have some, but it will be shorter. It will look really nice,' replied Josi. He was not convinced, especially as he pulled one of the ringlets in his afro and looked at himself in the mirror on the wall next to the bath.

Sometimes It's Funny

Ah, yes — the hair-washing routine was on again. I closed the door — to focus, of course, not to block out that particular dance — and continued working. It was — was it not? — a precious bonding moment between mother and son.

That record, I had heard many times before. I knew how it started, with my taking out the plaits or the cornrows while he was eating breakfast in the kitchen. We did not realise the booster seat had so many helpful multi-uses. Nowhere on its brief instructions did it say, 'Useful when needing to comb out afro hair.' I would not tell the manufacturer for fear they might increase the price for that additional function. The army of fathers and mothers yet to come should surely benefit from this secret advantage.

There were the inevitable complaints while I took out his hair, particularly to 'do it softer, like Mama.'

'I am, Jahdiel. I'm doing it very softly,' I repeat as my hands continue the task at the same pace: slow or fairly slow.

I played songs on the radio, on the phone, anywhere. Music everywhere, singing a medley of nursery rhymes, contemporary songs and new songs, asking, 'Do you know that one, Jahdiel?' Anything to distract from the comb as it made its steady way through his flowing locks. My cup of tea balanced precariously on the tabletop next to the cooker. I became accustomed to knowing when I could sneak sips, timing it so the tea would get cold just as I finished the

Every Hair on Your Head

last strand of hair. I was not yet proficient enough to work a slice or two of toast into the balancing act.

I was not sure whose relief was greater when I was done. Jahdiel all but bounced away as though he had been chained to the seat and had to grab his chance at freedom now; now, before some other cruel and unusual punishment breaching the Human Rights Act was performed on him.

I swept the residues of war from under the seat and took the chance to clear the whole kitchen from any specs of dirt. There was renewed vigour as the sweeping task was repeated as if my own newfound freedom needed an outlet.

Later, I heard Jahdiel playing somewhere in the house. Screams of delight. The best kind, I think. Morning screams of delight. Lovely, pure, as they came with the new day. A laughter of possibilities. A new morning, fresh with possibilities. We should all open the day with such excitement, running from room to room as sleep has fully recharged the batteries. No top-up would be required then. It added to the beautiful expectation of what the day would bring. Screams of delight turned to squeals of bliss as the water in the bath rose higher and higher, making its journey to the optimum level for bath time and, more importantly, today, hair-washing day.

His hair had not been cut since he was born. He also kept the texture of his just-born hair for a long time, it seemed. Someone took it upon themselves to give that just-born hair various hairstyles. As Granddad would say when looking at the guilty party, 'I am not mentioning any names, but look at my eyes.'

Yes, that was me in the mirror.

As the weeks and months passed, the afro got bigger and bigger. It had become clear that the top half of his hair was from Papa's family and the back from Mama's. I sought to banish any ideas of labelling one part 'good hair' with the implication of its corollary, that the other part was 'bad hair'. It was all lovely, just different in parts. The hair continued to transition on some journey known only to it.

Then, the steady process of Josi transforming his hair into cornrows and plaits, started. It had to. His afro was getting too large to simply leave for fear of irredeemable entanglement. It had gone beyond cute to chaos. So, at three and half years old, he had a beautiful afro when it was free of the cornrows, plaits or twists, thick, spongy and wide. That was its state when it was combed out before the washing routine.

With the cornrows, plaits and twists came the washing and greasing beforehand, as sure as night followed day, in preparation for the beautiful hairstyles created by Mama. Would it be cornrows that week? Plaits? Twists? Was that cornrows and plaits I saw? Not too tight, or they would pull. Not too loose, or they would not stay. It was a delicate balance for which seemingly dire consequences would

Every Hair on Your Head

flow if you strayed too far on the wrong side. Crying or discomfort could ensue. Silent tears could beckon that the cornrows had to be redone or touched up all too soon.

The hair routine was a work of hours, so it was only right that photograph after photograph was sent to family and friends over the months and years, evidencing the hair chronicles. More recently, though, there was a warning flying across the airwaves along with the photographs: enjoy it while it lasted, folks. Hair today, gone tomorrow.

I could not strongly empathise with his hair chronicles, having parted company with the hair on my own head many years ago. It had been a very long time since I'd campaigned at A-Level college that the boys with hair like mine should be allowed to have it cropped short if they wanted, not forced to keep a semi-afro. Level one or two haircut. 'We're not in the 1970s anymore,' I said to the teachers, thinking it really encapsulated how all the boys like me felt and surely, nothing more needed to be said.

Why endure the hair drama? Why not just chop it off? There was a cultural practice back home in Saint Lucia not to cut the hair of children until they could speak fluently. I heard some say, without any scientific evidence, that there were some children who got their hair cut too early, and it seemed to have later affected their way with words. I wonder if that had some kind of genesis with Samson from the Bible. The idea that if you cut his hair, it took away some of his strength. Would we be Delilah to Jahdiel's Samson, having discovered the secret of his strength and using that precious information to our own end?

Whatever the reality, we decided to keep from cutting Jahdiel's hair until he was speaking more fluently. It seemed to me he had already been speaking at an appropriate level for some time, and the flowing locks could be consigned to film, but that was an adventure yet to come.

Planning for that event, I am on the number 68 bus, looking out for barbers able to cut the hair of a child with an afro to a standard that would suit both him and us. As I look out the window, I wonder where the pieces that feed into his individuality will come from. My eyes run over the trees that periodically line the road, strategically placed or strategically left. Trees that Jahdiel will never climb. As is often the case, such thoughts transport me back to Saint Lucia.

Aunty Dawn and I, climbed fruit trees as young children, along with our cousins and friends in Desruisseaux, Keisha, Lyndon, Al and Jason, who joined us. We even tried those that should not be climbed, like trees overhanging the river and too willowy to support our weight. The coconut tree—so tall, so skinny, so daunting—was one tree none of us dared try to climb. Like the main road, like our older cousin, Ascenta's, bedroom, there were places even the adventurous members of the clan dared not go.

A favourite tree was the large mango tree, lower down the slope behind Mama's pre-school. It was so easy to climb, even our dog, Crystal, could reach the lower bower. As reading became a passion for me and Aunty Dawn in those very young years (strongly fostered by our mother), both of us came to see ourselves as Enid Blyton's folk of the Faraway Tree. That large mango tree became our Faraway Tree, and we gave each member of our adventurous clan names from the book, as we became the folk.

Those foundations helped build the individual that I am. I want Jahdiel to have the best chance to develop into himself and be who he is meant to be, when his lived experiences will be so different from my own. Experiences like those I had in Saint Lucia as a child will not feed into his individuality. Or if they do, it will only be in an indirect way. There's a degree of sadness for me in that, but I have to trust in the process of Jahdiel's reality when building who he is.

All children are special and unique. Precious, fragile beings. So individual. They have all been put here on this earth for a specific reason. They all have a job to do, to fulfil their life's calling. Through all that and more, how could we not want to love and protect them while they build their own moments and memories, though they will be different from our own.

Sometimes It's Funny

Josi's Reflections

In Montserrat, we had similar, traditional views about not cutting the hair of boys for a few years. There were many tales of when my male cousins and my brother's hair were cut for the first time as toddlers. There were tales of tears from toddlers, the stern, uncompromising faces of parents and pity from the onlookers. Those stories have started to take on the feel of folk tales. Grandma said my brother, Uncle Des, cried before, during and after his haircutting experience. Indeed, some kept on growing their hair. Did something in those early years of haircutting contribute to whether or not some boys in the family kept their cornrows well into their teenage years and beyond? With all that, it is no wonder I have hesitated many times when thinking about cutting Jahdiel's hair.

Before cutting comes the challenge of combing and plaiting. As one of the youngest cousins growing up in Montserrat, the older cousins often plaited, braided or cornrowed my hair. I never had to do the plaiting. And so, my experience when building that skill—which is what it really is—came from my playful attempts at combing and plaiting my grandmother's hair. Such a skill never properly learnt, it fostered apprehension as to how I would plait my own daughter's hair if the baby was a girl. I completely forgot that, in the first few years of babies' lives, the hair chronicles did not differ much between boys and girls.

And so, as Jahdiel started out with large, crooked plaits and cornrows, I saw the laughter in those cousins' eyes, though they were too polite to laugh out loud. Or maybe they could see that I was still nestled in the 'Sleep Chapter' of my parenting experience and thought better of saying anything on the subject. As the months passed and the hair art got better, I saw applause in those same cousins' eyes.

There is cultural judgement if a child leaves the home with their hair in an inappropriate state. Even if you, the parent, do not look your best, as long as the children are well-presented, hair and clothes, it is all right. As was said to me, 'He needs to look like somebody's child.'

He has to be. His hair has to be suitable for nursery, church, any outside activities. And so, I mentally prepared myself for his regular hair routine, though it could take hours with the washing, combing and cornrows. A half day was set aside.

I was gentle with Jahdiel, as I well-remembered the robustness with which my own hair was combed in Montserrat. Quiet tears might have come zig-zagging down the face of my young self, but I knew then that my head had better be kept still and straight.

Seeing him with all that hair makes it hard to imagine him with short hair. And so, again, I hesitated when thoughts of cutting came to mind. That hair seemed so much a part of him. How would he look without it? Did that also mean he was growing out of the baby stage and, however he may feel about it, was I ready for it?

After I finished his hair, even after all the drama, he toddled over and admired himself in the large mirror in the hallway downstairs, touching the twists, turning this way and that to see the finished product. In time, when he was able, he would say, 'Thank you, Mama, for doing my hair.' Should I cut short those memories along with the cutting of his hair?

Educating those around us in London who did not look like us but, more importantly, were ignorant of our cultural norms, that carried its own allocation of time, much more than half the day.

'Yes, we do have to put grease in his hair for moisture, which is somewhat different to yours.'

'No, he does not have head lice. His scalp is just dry, and that is why he is scratching it.' The lice comb did not really work on afro hair, anyway.

'No, he is not a girl. He is just a handsome boy with plaits.' How many times did I have to say that or some variety of it?

Sometimes, we had to resist the thought of getting his hair cut just to avoid all of that nonsense because there were already enough battles to fight.

Every Hair on Your Head

To cut or not to cut.

When the haircutting conversation came up again, Jahdiel asked who he would look like. The hair on Papa's head is razored low, so there was no comparison there. 'Will I look like M or N?' he asked about friends from nursery who did not have the same hair texture as his.

'It will be short, Jahdiel, but it will not look like theirs. You will look like you, handsome.'

As with hair, so with life, Jahdiel. In so many ways, you are like your friends, but in many important ways, you are different, too, and that is great. You are all different, all of you, and that is as it should be. You will look like yourself, Jahdiel. Unique. Psalms 139:14 KJV puts it perfectly: for I am fearfully and wonderfully made.

Is It Enough?

Though their beginning was small, yet their latter end should greatly increase.
– **Job 8:7 KJV**

WE STOOD WAVING. Nursery seemed a distant memory; he got out. It was a crisp, late summer morning, and Jahdiel went in for his first day of pre-reception education at his school. It was a bright morning. If we cared to check, if we were not consumed by the moment, we could have gone to even higher ground and seen for miles.

The school was firmly ensconced behind a church. The narrow entry to the school belied the bounteous brilliance of the school's grounds. From the road, you could not see the lovely playground, the interweaving classrooms caused by the juxtaposition of the old building against the new. Or pause to appreciate the small woodland behind the school. We would later learn about Woodland Dash from Jahdiel. Later we will hear about the learning around the fire pit, the joy of feeling as if he were in the country in London. It was a thing of beauty, but we didn't hear of his enjoyment of this until much later.

For the time being, we stood, waving, reflecting back on the journey that brought us to that point. We tried not to weigh the moment with the full spectrum of expectations. We tried not to make it mean more than it did or should, but attempting to do that was all nonsense because the moment spoke for itself. It was the culmination of where we all were thus far. Sometimes, it was funny, yes, but a lot of the time, we did not see the humour at the time. It was intense at times, frivolous at other times.

We wondered whether our journey to grey hair was accelerated, and I wondered whether there weren't a few strands of hair on my head that had said goodbye for good. We did not dare try for perfection, whatever that might be, but it would, again, be nonsense to suggest we did not aim for perfection, however far it might have been on the distant horizon. Ultimately, we wondered if we were doing enough.

As if it picked up on what was going on in our heads, the weather did not seem to know whether to be calm or entertain a windy gale. There were grey clouds on the horizon. We were not sure if it meant there was rain to

Is It Enough

come or if it was a trick of the light. Rays of sun cut through the grey clouds if that is what they were, and they started to dissipate. Our moistened eyes reflected how much that moment in time touched us.

Jahdiel knew the gravity of that part of his life's journey. At only three and a half years old, before we arrived at school, he had told us, 'When I go to school, I'm going to cry and say, "I want Mama and Papa."' He demonstrated how he would cry: 'Sniff, sniff.' He demonstrated that he would show just the right amount of sadness with his head down at exactly the right angle. He smiled at us to ensure we knew that his performance would be great. Like so many other times, he made us turn our heads away and laugh. He lightened the mood in case we took ourselves too seriously.

'You are going to enjoy school, Jahdiel. You're not going to do that.' Josi said.

He just repeated the performance.

So said, so done; he began to perform when we started to leave him in the classroom.

We waved again and swiftly left the school grounds. He will be okay, we thought and said to each other. It was not a question; it could not be. It was, as it needed to be, a statement of fact.

We walked off for home, hand in hand. It was another date walk. You had to grab the moments when you could, right up there with date shopping. We were quiet for a period of time as we walked, hand in hand, letting the moment marinate in our heads and go in whatever direction it chose to go. He would be fine.

Later, I called my parents, who were on holiday in Saint Lucia. My father — Granddad to Jahdiel — picked up the phone.

'Hi, Granddad — what are you doing today?'

'The usual. Nothing,' Granddad said with a drawl. I often asked Granddad why he was not doing some gardening or getting involved in the Men's Group at church. Or... well, the countless little chores and events you'd expect of those who are no longer working.

His answer was always the same. I could picture him, arms stretched out to either side, palms up, shoulders raised, with a smile on his face, intoning, 'I'm retired.' That, it seemed, was meant to explain it all. And it did.

We ultimately wanted Jahdiel to be able to make that choice when he got to retirement, to choose to do the fullness of nothing.

When I put the telephone down, it brought to mind a stinging comment Aunty Dawn once made about an acquaintance: 'He has no ambition. I don't think he has much up there. Or if he's intelligent, he must be really hiding it.' We would not want anyone to think this of Jahdiel. Even more importantly, we would not want him to think that of himself. We would like him to be the best self he can be.

Is It Enough

I do not require him to be a mini-Papa—what I want for myself, I will do for myself. I do not wish to project onto him any unfulfilled dreams and aspirations I may have. Hopefully, our children will be able to do the things our parents could not do because the world would not let them. Hopefully our parents having done enough for us, we can continue the doing of enough for our own children.

Have we done enough to equip him for this world? Is that a worry of every parent? Will his roots remain firm, deep and strong enough to withstand any storm? And there will be many. It is too much to ask that there be no storms. That is not realistic, is it? There have to be trials and tribulations. In the fire will he be forged. Iron sharpens iron.

So, we do not ask for no storms. We will continue to be Jahdiel's advocates in areas of life where we might have remained quiet if it were for ourselves. There are areas opened—worlds opened—because of his existence, which we may never have known about. We must be his advocates until he is ready to take up the mantle himself. Though we doubt we will stop, even then.

I am catapulted back to secondary school in London, where I remember a disturbing comment from an older student. It was an alright school. Being Roman Catholic, it had degrees of discipline that I appreciate now, which were helpful. An all-boys school, the complex conundrum of making my way through five years in a challenging part of London was not further complicated by having to deal with girls in school. It was one of those schools where the students put 'kick me' signs on teachers' backs, where you could do well if you were intelligent or savvy, preferably both, where you were okay if you were smart enough, where you were likely lost if you were none of those things.

Survived, I did — lessons learned — but I was not, I think, unscathed. An older boy came up to me in the hallway during one break time. I had no idea who he was, but too shy to do anything else, I stopped and listened as he spoke. He clearly knew of me. Perhaps he knew me as the boy who'd told the teacher she had a 'kick me' sign on her back. Maybe he'd seen me from a distance, a part of the masses who'd ostracised me for a week for betraying some code that I, innocent and ignorant that I was, had no idea I had breached.

'Why are you working so hard?' He sought to educate me. 'Don't you know you're Black?' He completed his lesson with a worried look on his face.

It was all the more disturbing said, as it was, by a boy who looked like me in a school full of students who looked like us. He told me this, looking concerned that he had to inform me of the blindingly obvious. The look on his face made it clear that he was baffled he had to explain this cardinal truth to the clearly uninitiated, a truth as unwavering and as known as gravity. Whatever I was doing

Is It Enough

troubled his world, and I wondered whether he thought there would be unhelpful repercussions for that world. Maybe it was a warning, he thought helpful, believing I was going in a direction that would lead me to... what? Disappointment? Regret?

Wisdom bestowed, he walked away from me, mixing with the crowd of students. The exchange hardly lasted a minute, but it resonated.

We didn't want Jahdiel to be the kind of young man who would make such a comment, nor did we want him to be one to whom such a comment would be made, because we wanted that world to be long in the past. Much more, though, we wanted him to be the kind of young man who knew how to respond to such a statement, who could respond much better than I did. I was probably in shock and did not know what to say, so my 12-year-old self said nothing.

My memories tumble forward in time. I used to read in church, thrust forward by the priest who'd selected me — I do not know why — for the task of reading. I am actually grateful to him as from that time on, I read regularly at church.

One Sunday service, after the usual reading, a little old lady who did not look like me came up to me and said, 'You read so well.' A smile came to my face. Ah, the acknowledgement of the congregation — how kind.

'When I used to work in the prisons, the Jamaican men couldn't speak very well at all,' she continued.

Did I just hear that correctly? I put aside the fact that I am not Jamaican. I am not sure how church parallels prison either, but I put that aside, too. In the moment, I think it is probably inappropriate to tell an elderly person what I would really like to say. Her advanced years would probably resist the education I wished to force on her anyway.

Saying nothing, I searched deeply for the scintilla of a compliment buried deep in her proclamation.

We want Jahdiel to be able to do more than my inaction. To have his amour ready and to learn, as I did, from such events. It did not stop me from continuing to read in church, and it helped my blinkers come off a little.

Further forward in time. The court usher smiled benignly at me and asked, 'Will you be represented today?'

Really? It was 2020, so, really? What was it that strongly suggested that I was not counsel myself? Was it my black suit and tie? Was it my black overcoat? Was it the bag laden with my tablet, laptop and other modern lawyer paraphernalia? Was it the clean-shaven face (head and beard)?

'I *am* the representation,' I informed him.

'Oh, sorry, sorry,' was his bashful reply.

My blinkers, which I still had on, unbeknownst to me, were starting to come off even more. Or maybe it was the obviousness of the situation that could not help but resonate and penetrate. We did not want Jahdiel to be blinkered.

What do you do about your client in court when he calls you 'boy' (would that be a capital or lowercase 'b' I ask myself) when you are just fighting the good fight so he will have contact with his child? There really is no silver-lining-way to interpret that.

We do not want our son to be referred to as 'boy', but if he is, we want him to have his intellectual weapons ready. We want to improve this world in whatever small ways we can to insulate Jahdiel from such experiences. We want him to have the choice and right to study creative subjects like the History of Art at university. To be free from the choice of the Trio—lawyer, doctor or other.

Have we done enough?

I had a conversation with Jahdiel when he was the grand old age of three years and nine months young.

'Papa, is it funny?' he asked.

I forget the context, but remember my reply: 'It is, Jahdiel.'

So much is so serious in the dance of life. Laughter is so important. He needs to know how to laugh. That deep belly laugh where you roll around on the floor because you cannot hold it in, laughing so much that tears come to your eyes, and you cannot hear anything, you cannot see anything, and there is no sense of gravity. A delight so exquisite it hurts! Aunty Dawn will remember that laugh for herself when she was present for Jahdiel's preaching Hallelujah in the front room as he pranced around with his toy microphone.

Studies have proven the benefits of laughter for physical, mental, emotional and psychological health and the release of endorphins. So many times, we would be travelling to one place or another and burst into laughter at something hilarious Jahdiel said or did that came to mind. The people around us probably thought there was something wrong with us. Actually, there was something very right with us at those times. Transported back as we were to those blissful, laughter-inducing moments, we wanted the joy to be contagious. It reminded us about being the joy we wanted to see in others. It brought to mind Jahdiel as a baby when he first started to laugh.

***

After a long day of work away from home, I approached the front door of our house. The forceful expression of air from my mouth encapsulated the whole day from the time I'd left that front door in the morning. I kissed my teeth as an exclamation mark. It was a condensing of all the many things on my To-Do list, the many people I had met who I challenged or who challenged me, the wonderful moments and those heavily laden with frustration.

Is It Enough

Opening the door, I saw Jahdiel sitting in the living room with Josi. Her smile is mirrored on Jahdiel's face as he runs to me, cornrows in disarray from the activity of the day. 'Papa!' he exclaimed, his arms wide open as he jumped, full speed, into my arms. My smile made it three as I spun him around and gave him a hug that said everything. His gleeful energy was a welcome breeze. I demanded my dance from Josi. She smiled, walked towards us and complied.

All of the nonsense faded away, shelved. For the time being, it would have to be enough.

Josi's Reflections

EDWARD KNOCKED ON THE FRONT DOOR, AND JAHDIEL BOUNCED UP. 'Papa,' he said.

I watched as he ran, full speed towards Edward, and I contemplated, not for the first time, the wonder of him. I watched him with a smile because every time he ran to Edward at the end of the day, just like that, it was as if it was the very first time he was seeing his father. A part of it was for him, of course, but another part was for Edward. I had my moments of hugging and kissing Jahdiel all the time, so it was heart-warming to see their connection.

I thought back to my early days of working in a corporate setting. I needed to make so many adjustments. Most of my work colleagues just needed to concern themselves with excelling, but I had to grapple with their world as well as strive to excel; two full-time jobs to their one, it seemed at times.

We want Jahdiel to own himself enough that he does not feel out of place or intimidated by situations or the people around him. It cannot be that he feels small in those environments, nor should he feel the need to adjust himself. In his confidence, he has to know that he can excel without needing to consciously think about it. We do not want Jahdiel to feel the need to change himself or his sense of self. Was that a struggle for all of us, feeling the need to tone ourselves down depending on the situation?

We want Jahdiel to occupy and fill the spaces he navigates. To do so without needing to even think about it. We have surely done all the thinking already, all the wondering of whether we belonged in the spaces we occupied. Have we done enough so that he does not need to engage himself in such deep contemplation? That is such a big question. What are the indicators of success in having done enough?

Did you go by the comments of parents who said Jahdiel gravitated to children who needed to settle in? He helped them. Or the judgement of the school telling us about the great things Jahdiel does? Or should we go by what

Is It Enough

FamilyFriends said about him? Were they the barometer? Or was it just what we, as parents, saw in our day-to-day lives with him, however the world might test it?

It is a harsh world out there, and we want to protect him, or at least help him have the tools to take his place in the world. Not in his own strength, but in His strength.

We hope we have done enough, whatever the standard, for him to move to the next stage, then the battle will continue, no doubt, as we keep trying to do enough. As we keep looking to what more we can and should do.

For now, in the moment in the living room, we are really living. Jahdiel has reached Edward and is being spun around. My smile brightened. I parked my contemplations and joined them for our dance.

...With Thanks

*Encourage each other and build each other up... Always be joyful.
Never stop praying. Be thankful in all circumstances.*
– 1 Thessalonians 5:11; 16-18 NLT

Thank God for bringing us this far. If You brought us to it, You will bring us through it! Let us not be ashamed of our faith. *For whosoever shall be ashamed of me and my words, of him shall the son of man be ashamed* (Luke 9:26 KJV). So many times you have to dig deep from the Source to take you through.

It really is unfair to name only certain people as there are so many who have been a part of this journey in different ways, either knowingly or unknowingly. Even some we are not aware of ourselves. However, it would be nonsense not to mention a few precious gems, and we are only sorry we cannot mention everyone. Really, we have to name and proclaim because the support network is and has been a vitally important part of this journey, so this section of the book comes not as an afterthought but as a chapter in its own right, with thanks.

Wherever the proverb *it takes a village to raise a child* comes from, it encapsulates the situation well. It can be very disappointing to realise you are not superhuman. Although, even with that realisation, you harbour a feeling lodged deep within the grey matter that actually, you still are superhuman. The mathematics though just do not work out when you try to give 100% to the family, 100% to work and 100% to the rest of life's journey. A good friend once told Edward that he gave a good solid 20% percent to his family when he was working. Whatever amount of energy you give, you really do need to share the load with the village, or something will give way. So, we will share some of our village with you.

A big thanks to Aunty Dawn, Dr Anneline Flood, for reading an initial draft of this book and generally supporting us through this and other journeys. It is truly a blessing to have a sister like you. There is no one who will fight for you more than Aunty Dawn. Edward has said it before, and he will say it again: you are the best sister in the world.

To Grandmama Menna Flood and Granddad Pierre Quinlan Flood for their constant support in all areas.

...With Thanks

Grandmama, you really are amazing for all you do for everyone. You always said you work for your children and heat. Our hearts are immensely lightened after our conversations with you. As we and you always say, thanks for all you do. Granddad, your quiet support and pride have been felt like the rippling heat in your beloved Doden.

To Grandma Joicelyn Daley: it is sometimes when you stand in your parents' shoes that you understand—really understand—what they have done for you. It is often only then you fully appreciate all the ways, often small, that they have prepared you for this life's journey. Grandpa Desmond 'Flasha' Daley, you have paved the way for us in so many ways. You got to put pen to paper first! No doubt, Jahdiel probably got his musical talent through you.

People really should not underestimate how invaluable grandparents are. We see them taking their grandchildren to school. The juxtaposition of boundless energy and verve wanting to burst out of the toddler and the calm, slower, personification of wisdom that is embodied in Grandma or Grandpa. The childcare allowing the elusive date night. The secret sweet treats parents fear will lead to the little ones catching an early train; ultimate destination, dentures. The secret army of grandparents for whom love is payment enough. Even then, going one step further to finance the ever-increasing cost of children. To grandparents everywhere, we salute you.

Aunty Sha (Sharon Daley Martin), you have waited many years to see this child, Jahdiel. It is so right that you and Grandma were two of the first ones to embrace him at our home shortly after he was born. Josi will never forget how you kept her focused and grounded amidst a sea of pressures to have a baby soon after marriage. You were a constant reassurance that it would happen at the right time, and that we needed to enjoy our marriage. What can we say, Aunty Sha? You are a gem.

Uncle Des, Aunty Trudy and Cousin Niah, we value the many times we have been able to meet up as a family. Uncle Des, for your continuing plans to get the family together, we salute and thank you. We have great respect for you, Uncle Des. Your excitement about having a nephew was enough to ensure that we delivered that gift to you! Aunty Princess, Aunty P, you kept making Edward smile and laugh during the journey, keeping him buoyed up, completely unbeknownst to you. As he said, Aunty P, you should do a podcast! Aunty Len (Pastor Lenore Greenaway), the mere fact that Jahdiel runs to you for a jumping hug whenever he sees you really says it all. Aunty Jackie (Jaqueline Greenaway), for all the reminders of cultural remedies and practices, when we just did not know what to do or what we were doing, we are so grateful.

Thanks to Keisha Athil for proofreading and giving us a useful overview and perspective of Saint Lucia. Keish,

...With Thanks

what you do not know about Saint Lucia probably is not worth knowing! You were there in the Faraway Tree. You were a part of the adventures in Saint Lucia when Edward and Aunty Dawn were children. We hope those memories are as precious to you as they are to Edward. Albina Augustin, Aunty Bin, you have been such a strong supporter of the three of us. Offering to babysit and toddler sit and dropping off food when neither of us could face the cooker, but most importantly, your levity and jokes could keep anyone buoyed up. Sharing your own experiences of raising children (three, no less!) helped put things in a much-needed perspective. Those stories really helped epitomise that sometimes situations with our children are really belly-aching, tear-inducing, roll around on the floor funny!

Felicity Chame (*Nennenn*) and Dr Andrew Meso (*Pawen*). Thank you for being godparents in more than just name, which was the whole point! *Nennenn*, your continued support began pre-Jahdiel, and now that you are fully on board assuming the mantle, we hope that godmotherhood is not too heavy. There are bridges we would not have been able to cross without you. Indeed, sometimes you were the one to point out that the bridge existed at all! Simmone Zachariah (Aunty Sissy), how could we do anything but praise you and thank you for the many facets of our journey on which you have walked with us and danced with us, including at the wedding? You are the embodiment of a stalwart supporter. Aunty G (Germaine Dolcy), Edward well remembers that brilliant Christmas holiday when Aunty Dawn and Edward were fully ensconced in your home, left and came back. Those kinds of memories are enough to keep anyone buoyed, they are springboards to our smiles and our laughter. We thanked you at our wedding and underline those thanks now.

Sabrina Williams, Aunty Bree, we really appreciated your taking the time from your multi-juggling to give us some thoughts on the draft. You have been such a supporter all the way. It was such a brilliant conversation when Edward told you about the book and asked you to put your touch on it. Just our laughter alone, talking it through, really showed what an undiluted brilliant person you are. Tears danced in Edward's eyes from your comments during the WhatsApp exchanges while you were reading the draft! Those great exchanges were like taking family and friends from abroad to visit tourist attractions where you live. You may have seen those tourist attractions before, but they come to life again through new eyes. You kept making the book come alive to Edward again and again. That was really needed sometimes.

Edward's three best men, Dr Edney Boston-Griffiths, Dr David Drysdale and Daniel Dawes J. D., we stand by all that was said about you gentlemen at our wedding. You do not need loads of pebbles, just a few strong rocks. You are rocks. We do not and should not walk this life's journey

...With Thanks

alone. You gentlemen help make it a pleasure. You each know yourselves, which is not a small thing. Edney, you remain an all-round inspiration, including the way you try to shape cardiological wellness for your clients. Your nuggets of wisdom continue to sit with Edward. David, your frank, no-nonsense conversations, which inevitably involve some degree of humour, are frankly a powerful force. Daniel, your work ethic is incredible. You make us want to push, strive, achieve more. It is such a pleasure whenever we speak, and it is right that, through your books, you are shared with the world.

The Boys Collective: Real Boys Foundation (RBF): John Anthony MBE, Jonathan Anthony, Alfred Bentil, Dr Edney Boston-Griffiths, Gareth Burke, Dr Gordon Burke, Dr Andrew Meso and Osita Okereafor—harnessing our power would make something even more amazing. You are a collective inspiration, making great strides in your respective spheres. Gentlemen, we really do salute you all.

The village it takes to raise a child has firmly included the elegant Sister Christenelda Walters (Nanny Walters). Where would we be without your delicious and delightful dinners, the tasty treats and wonderful company? Mummy Joan (Joan Tuitt), Uncle Phil (Philemon Tuitt) and Daddy Woodley (Augustus Woodley), there is a whole book on its own that would try (and fail) to cover all the support you three have provided to us. To Josi first, before Edward came along, then to us as a couple. Prayer warrior Mummy Joan, it is so comforting when someone undiluted, unreservedly, without stain or conditions, without caveats, has your best interests at heart. Daddy Woodley, we need your nuggets immortalised. The world needs the benefit of your wisdom and insights. Brother Victor Moore and Sister Anne Moore, what can we say? Your daily devotion posts, your prayers, have been uplifting, and you as a couple have been inspiring. We miss you, Sister Moore. Sister Lusta Morson, *merci put tout sa ou faire.*

To Charles and Sheuli Ankrah for their invaluable support. Charlie, you know the conversations you have had with Edward about this journey and other things. The laughter has been deep, long and gratifying. You really are quite amazing, Charlie. Pamela Warner—yes, we will name you as we really cannot but do so, Pam, so superb a friend and confidante you are. You have also been a sounding board for the book for a long time. Thank you for your guidance, your wisdom and your discretion. A shout out loud to Vernette and Darren John Joiles: V, you know, we hope, where you both lie in our hearts. For the constant humour, especially the big reveal of your attending our wedding, makes us smile, even now.

Shannon Pite, thank you for your help in sourcing research for some sensitive issues. That you were able to take the time from your extremely busy work and life

...With Thanks

schedule is really appreciated. Reach Out to Kids (ROK) needs more people like you. We all do. Our thanks, indeed, to Edward's entire ROK family, with Denise Stephenson at the helm. ROK has done such great work, it cannot help but be inspirational, not just in the work we have done for young people of colour, but to show how we can and should give back to this world. It is incumbent on us to give back when we can, to try to make this world a better place and have such fun doing it! Denise, you are simply an amazing woman; you really are.

Edward feels driven to mention Sister Sarah, his mathematics teacher at secondary school. Sister Sarah would glide down the hallowed halls of the school, and everyone—students, teachers and other staff—would part the way in front of her like Moses parting the Red Sea as she looked straight ahead, fixed on her destination. There might be the barest of nods and the smallest of smiles to a few along the journey who were fortunate enough to be so graced. Not many were. Looking back now, that force, which was Sister Sarah really helped Edward on his journey of accumulating confidence.

Others who may have had no idea that we are grateful to them include Bebe's dad Neil, who, unbeknownst to him, helped us see how it was done and done well. Pastor Lewis and Sister Lewis, in so many ways, not the least of which is leading the good ship Shiloh Pentecostal Church.

Little Molly—not so little now—who showed us signs of where confidence can lie. Thanks for her, Leah. That special practitioner who came to our rescue when despair started to set in at the nursery. Aunty Val and Uncle Sam, who we were allowed to borrow for toddler-sitting duties. Sarah Morgan for the treats and who is the one who said of Jahdiel that he was appropriately suspicious of the world. To Bishop John Francis and Co-pastor Penny Francis from Ruach City Church for their inspiration via live streaming. Sometimes, people need to know the positive impact they have. To Brother Dean Allert and his graceful wife, Sister Gracita Allert, for being who they both are and for their energy, which they passed on to others through osmosis.

To the Lashleys for their constant support and for sometimes letting Jahdiel borrow Amber! To Sister Carmen Donaldson, who whispered to Edward in a friendly, conspiratorial voice all those years ago as she made her way round church to give her offering: 'The wedding must be soon'. That offering from her, so beautifully packaged and said, was welcomed with joy. Thank you, Sister Carmen, for confirming even before Edward proposed, what we knew must be done.

For all those who were kind enough to read drafts of the book and even kinder in giving constructive feedback rather than shaking their heads in consternation! And those with whom we discussed this baby. In particular, we simply

...With Thanks

cannot leave without mentioning, saluting and thanking Christy Grigg, who helped transform this endeavour from our project to something that could be released, and Rebecca Mitchell, who connected us. Christy, you helped us see that what was in our heads need not just stay there!

To all of you very dear readers, we say thanks. We hope you enjoyed experiencing this book as much as we enjoyed the wonder of helping it come into being.

Edward & Josi

... and Jahdiel

About the Authors

Photo credit Tee Max insta @teedilla71

EA Flood and JA Flood were raised on the Caribbean islands of Saint Lucia and Montserrat during their formative years. They have spent most of their time living in London, where they met – an interesting story in itself. They married in Saint Lucia and continue to reside in London with their son, Jahdiel. 'Sometimes It's Funny: Adventures in Parenthood' is their first book.

Conscious Dreams
PUBLISHING

Transforming diverse writers
into successful published authors

www.consciousdreamspublishing.com

authors@consciousdreamspublishing.com

Let's connect

www.ingramcontent.com/pod-product-compliance
Lightning Source LLC
Chambersburg PA
CBHW030323080526
44584CB00012B/679